Modern Cryptography for Cybersecurity Professionals

Learn how you can leverage encryption to better secure your organization's data

Lisa Bock

BIRMINGHAM—MUMBAI

Modern Cryptography for Cybersecurity Professionals

Copyright © 2021 Packt Publishing

Group Product Manager: Wilson D'souza

Publishing Product Manager: Rahul Nair

Senior Editor: Arun Nadar

Content Development Editor: Romy Dias

Technical Editor: Shruthi Shetty

Copy Editor: Safis Editing

Project Coordinator: Shagun Saini

Proofreader: Safis Editing

Indexer: Manju Arasan

Production Designer: Prashant Ghare

First published: May 2021

Production reference: 2140621

Published by Packt Publishing Ltd.

Livery Place

35 Livery Street

Birmingham

B3 2PB, UK.

ISBN 978-1-83864-435-2

www.packt.com

No one really knows how planes stay in the air. They do, however, know that lift, an aerodynamic force, allows them to take flight. I dedicate this book to all those that believed in me, had faith in my abilities, and gave me the lift to take off and excel in my field.

Contributors

About the author

Lisa Bock is an experienced author with a demonstrated history of working in the e-learning industry. She is a security ambassador with a broad range of IT skills and knowledge, including on Cisco Security, CyberOps, Wireshark, biometrics, ethical hacking, and IoT. Lisa is an author for LinkedIn Learning and an award-winning speaker who has presented at several national conferences. She holds an MS in computer information systems/information assurance from UMGC. Lisa was an associate professor in the IT department at Pennsylvania College of Technology (Williamsport, PA) from 2003 until her retirement in 2020. She is involved with various volunteer activities, and she and her husband Mike enjoy bike riding, watching movies, and traveling.

I'd like to thank Dr. Jacob Miller, long-time colleague at Pennsylvania College of Technology, who had the foresight to create an Information Assurance degree in 2003. His early effort exposed me to a field I genuinely love. In addition, I'd like to thank Anita Wood for her continued wisdom, advice, and ability to solve problems. Finally, I'd like to acknowledge the entire Packt editing team, who have helped me to become a better author, along with Product Manager Rahul Nair, with whom I have enjoyed collaborating over the years.

About the reviewer

Vipin Singh Sehrawat received his Ph.D. degree in computer science from The University of Texas at Dallas, USA, in 2019. He is currently working as Lead Cryptographer in the Data Security team of Seagate Research Group at Seagate Technology, Singapore. His research interests include cryptography, combinatorics, extremal set theory, information theory, number theory, software security, and network security.

Table of Contents

Section 2:
Understanding Cryptographic Techniques

4
Introducing Symmetric Encryption

Section 3:
Applying Cryptography in Today's World

7
Adhering to Standards

8
Using a Public Key Infrastructure

9
Exploring IPsec and TLS

10
Protecting Cryptographic Techniques

Assessments

Other Books You May Enjoy

Index

Preface

In today's world, it's important to have confidence while either transmitting or storing data. Cryptography can provide confidentiality, integrity, authentication, and non-repudiation. But just what exactly is involved when we use cryptographic techniques? *Modern Cryptography for Cybersecurity Professionals* will help you gain a better understanding of the cryptographic protocols and processes that are necessary to secure data.

We'll learn how encryption can protect data, whether in motion or at rest. You'll get a better understanding of symmetric and asymmetric encryption and learn how a hash is used. You'll also see how a public key infrastructure and certificates enable trust between parties, so we can confidently encrypt and exchange data. You'll then see the practical applications of cryptographic techniques, including passwords, email, and securely transmitting data using a **Virtual Private Network (VPN)**.

Who this book is for

This book is appropriate for IT managers, security professionals, students, teachers, or anyone who would like to learn more about cryptography and reasons it is important in an organization as part of an overall security framework. Participants should have a basic understanding of encryption, knowledge of general networking terms and concepts, and an interest in the subject.

What this book covers

Chapter 1, Protecting Data in Motion or at Rest, provides an overview of the current threat landscape. You'll learn how encryption provides many security services, such as confidentiality, integrity, and authentication. We'll then review some common terms, along with two basic cryptographic concepts: substitution and transposition.

Chapter 2, The Evolution of Ciphers, takes us through some early uses of cryptography. We'll review monoalphabetic and polyalphabetic ciphers and compare different methods used to encode transmissions during wartime. We'll then learn about the development of the Lucifer and Feistel ciphers, as scientists recognized the need to secure digital data.

Chapter 3, Evaluating Network Attacks, compares passive and active attacks and outlines why it's essential to protect data so that it remains in its original, unaltered form. You'll then learn how using encryption can ensure data integrity and prevent it from being changed, destroyed, or lost in an unauthorized or accidental manner.

Chapter 4, Introducing Symmetric Encryption, steps through the evolution of symmetric (or secret key) encryption. We'll examine common algorithms, such as the Advanced Encryption Standard. We'll then dissect block and stream ciphers and compare the different operating modes. Finally, we'll take a look at some methods of securing wireless communications.

Chapter 5, Dissecting Asymmetric Encryption, outlines how asymmetric (or public key) encryption can be used in many ways, such as exchanging the shared secret key, securing email, and creating a digital signature. We'll compare algorithms such as **Rivest, Shamir, Adleman** (**RSA**) and Diffie-Hellman, along with a discussion on key management.

Chapter 6, Examining Hash Algorithms, explains that a hash algorithm is a one-way function that produces a fixed-length output called a message digest. We'll identify some of the optimal hash properties along with some common hash algorithms in use today. Finally, you'll learn how a message digest provides message authentication.

Chapter 7, Adhering to Standards, explains that security laws and standards exist to provide guidelines and best practices to prevent data loss. In addition, we'll compare ways that we can use encryption to protect data, but also how cybercriminals use encryption to conceal malicious activity.

Chapter 8, Using a Public Key Infrastructure, outlines how the **Public Key Infrastructure** (**PKI**) framework provides trust between two entities communicating on the internet by using a trusted third party that enables secure interactions between entities. We'll discuss key management and examine what happens when both parties exchange a certificate.

Chapter 9, Exploring IPsec and TLS, combines all of your knowledge of cryptography as we examine the concepts of a VPN. We'll begin by outlining several types of VPNs in use today and explain the concept of an **Internet Protocol Security** (**IPsec**) VPN, along with a **Transport Layer Security** (**TLS**) communication stream.

Chapter 10, Protecting Cryptographic Techniques, reviews common attacks designed to alter the integrity of our data or systems. We'll recognize how the PKI can be attacked, which can negate trust. Finally, we'll see how advances in technology will require quantum-resistant algorithms to encrypt and secure our data.

To get the most out of this book

When reading *Modern Cryptography for Cybersecurity Professionals*, you will learn the basics of how we secure data using encryption. In order to fully understand the concepts, I have provided several links in each chapter for additional research, which I encourage you to visit.

In addition, I have provided links that take you to sites to see some applications available online. For example, we'll visit sites that show us how letter frequency analysis works, how a hash algorithm transforms text, and what Morse code sounds like.

So that you can follow along, it's best to have an up-to-date browser such as Chrome, Firefox, or Safari on a Windows, macOS, or Linux machine.

> **Important note**
>
> Any web pages or email addresses are fictional. Any correlation with any real entities is purely coincidental.

Most of the resources will be found online, however, there are a few chapters that I will use specialized software, such as:

In *Chapter 6, Examining Hash Algorithms*, we'll cover how you can easily run a checksum on any file by using 7-Zip. To obtain a copy of 7-Zip, go to `https://www.7-zip.org/`.

In *Chapter 9, Exploring IPsec and TLS*, we'll take a look at PuTTY, a free SSH client you can use on a Windows system to access a single other host via Telnet and **remote login** (**rlogin**). To obtain a copy of PuTTY, go to `https://www.putty.org/`.

I encourage you to go to the sites I have provided to supplement your knowledge.

Download the color images

We also provide a PDF file that has color images of the screenshots/diagrams used in this book. You can download it here: `http://www.packtpub.com/sites/default/files/downloads/9781838644352_ColorImages.pdf`.

Conventions used

There are a number of text conventions used throughout this book.

`Code in text`: Indicates code words in text, database table names, folder names, filenames, file extensions, pathnames, dummy URLs, user input, and Twitter handles. Here is an example: "The Nmap scan shows the open and listening ports on host `10.0.0.167`."

> **Tips or important notes**
> Appear like this.

Get in touch

Feedback from our readers is always welcome.

General feedback: If you have questions about any aspect of this book, mention the book title in the subject of your message and email us at `customercare@packtpub.com`.

Errata: Although we have taken every care to ensure the accuracy of our content, mistakes do happen. If you have found a mistake in this book, we would be grateful if you would report this to us. Please visit `www.packtpub.com/support/errata`, selecting your book, clicking on the Errata Submission Form link, and entering the details.

Piracy: If you come across any illegal copies of our works in any form on the Internet, we would be grateful if you would provide us with the location address or website name. Please contact us at `copyright@packt.com` with a link to the material.

If you are interested in becoming an author: If there is a topic that you have expertise in and you are interested in either writing or contributing to a book, please visit `authors.packtpub.com`.

Reviews

Please leave a review. Once you have read and used this book, why not leave a review on the site that you purchased it from? Potential readers can then see and use your unbiased opinion to make purchase decisions, we at Packt can understand what you think about our products, and our authors can see your feedback on their book. Thank you!

For more information about Packt, please visit `packt.com`.

Section 1: Securing Our Data

In this section, we'll take a look at the current threat landscape so that you can better understand the reasons why we need to secure our data. First we'll outline how encryption can protect the data, whether in motion or at rest, by providing security services, such as confidentiality, integrity, and authentication. We'll then take a brief look at the evolution of ciphers over time, along with the development of Lucifer and Feistel ciphers, as scientists recognized the need to secure digital data. Finally, we'll compare some of the various network attacks that can alter the integrity of our data.

This section comprises the following chapters:

- *Chapter 1, Protecting Data in Motion or at Rest*
- *Chapter 2, The Evolution of Ciphers*
- *Chapter 3, Evaluating Network Attacks*

1
Protecting Data in Motion or at Rest

We live in an exciting yet challenging time. Every second of the day there are zettabytes of data traveling over networks and the internet. Data is constantly being sent and received from our homes, cars, businesses, and billions of **Internet of Things (IoT)** devices. In this chapter, you'll gain an appreciation for the need to secure our data in a dynamic digital world. We'll begin with a brief look at how, over the past few decades, we have seen advances in technology that have resulted in more of our data being exchanged. Concurrent to the advances in technology, we have seen an increase in the type and amount of threats to our data.

So that you understand the many resources available on guidelines for ensuring our data is not compromised, we'll take a look at the *Security architecture for Open Systems Interconnection for CCITT applications*, also known as *X.800*. You'll learn how encryption provides many security services, which include ensuring confidentiality, integrity, authentication, forward secrecy, non-repudiation, and enhanced privacy guarantees. In addition, we'll outline some common cryptographic concepts, such as **Trusted Third Party (TTP)** and the **Public Key Infrastructure (PKI)**. We'll also cover how we use the story of Bob, Alice, and other personalities to help us understand complex technical concepts.

We'll then cover some basic encryption techniques. You'll see how using substitution or transposition can scramble data into an unreadable form that won't make sense unless you have the key to decrypt the message. In order to better understand substitution and transposition, we will discuss some illustrative examples that employ two basic ciphers, namely pigpen and rail fence. Finally, we'll outline some basic techniques, such as letter frequency analysis, which can be used to break some codes.

This chapter covers the following main topics:

- Outlining the current threat landscape
- Understanding security services
- Introducing common cryptographic concepts
- Outlining substitution and transposition

Outlining the current threat landscape

Over the past three decades, there has been substantial growth in the amount of digital data, both at rest and in transit. The digital wave has become an ocean of all types of data, such as email, movies, images, and tweets. With this growth comes the threat of attacks on our data, which we face on a daily basis.

In this section, we'll take a look at how our world has transformed with the adoption of digital technology, along with an overview of the current threat landscape.

Let's start with a look at the growth in digital information over the years.

Digitally transforming our world

In 1946, the world got a glimpse of the future. That was the year that the *Moore School of Electrical Engineering* of the *University of Pennsylvania* introduced the **Electronic Numerical Integrator and Computer (ENIAC)** system. The ENIAC was enormous, as it filled a room and was capable of performing calculations faster than any other computer at the time.

When computers first appeared, the cost to own and operate a system was extremely high. Ordinary citizens knew very little about computers. Due to their prohibitively large costs, computer systems were owned mainly by governments, industry, and universities. In 1980, the cost of a **gigabyte (GB)** hard drive was approximately $1.2 million. By 1990, the price was down to $8,000, and costs continued to decrease. As shown in the following graphic, from 1995 to 2000, the price of drives per GB went down substantially:

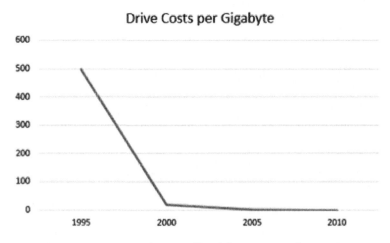

Figure 1.1 – The cost of hard drives per gigabyte

By 2010, the cost of drives per GB was approximately $0.10. Along with the cost of hard drives, the price of computers in general went down as well. With more affordable pricing, more and more businesses and consumers were embracing technology, as we'll see next.

Rapidly advancing technology

The industry continued to develop desktops, laptops, games, mobile devices, and IoT devices that began to collect and exchange more and more data. Concurrently, businesses, universities, governments, and consumers began to invest heavily in information technology, spending billions on hardware and software designed to improve the quality of life.

Today, a large percentage of the world is using digital technology and the internet, for a wide variety of purposes. Applications include e-commerce, social media, mobile banking, and email, all generating data.

Data includes anything you can see or hear and can be digitized in a multitude of different types and formats, including the following:

- **Voice over Internet Protocol (VoIP)**, also known as IP telephony, is a group of technologies primarily used to transmit phone calls over the internet
- Documents such as spreadsheets, word processor documents, presentation files, and **Portable Document Format (PDF)** files

- Images that include **Joint Photographic Group (JPG)**, **Tagged Image File Format (TIPP)**, and **Bitmap Image File (BMP)**

- Video that includes a wide range of formats, such as **Moving Picture Experts Group (MPEG)** and **Advanced Video Coding (AVC)**, originating from a variety of sources

Some may argue that not all data needs to be protected. However, much of the data that is in storage on a server or in motion while traveling across the network should be encrypted, mainly because this flood of data represents an opportunity for cybercriminals to obtain and exploit the data.

Every minute of every day, companies face a variety of threats to the security of their data. Let's explore this concept next.

Threatening the security of our data

Early systems, such as the ENIAC, were standalone systems and not networked. The biggest threat to these systems was a physical attack, such as someone destroying the components. As time passed, and businesses began to adopt computer technology, there still remained little threat to the security of data.

From the 1960s through to the 1990s, scientists developed protocols for the **Advanced Research Projects Agency Network (ARPANET)**, which was the precursor to what we know now as the internet. Some significant events during this time period include the following:

- 1972 – Ray Tomlinson creates electronic mail (email).

- 1973 – Scientists began to use the term *internet*.

- 1974 – The first **Internet Service Provider (ISP)** begins offering its service.

- 1982 – Formalization of **Transmission Control Protocol (TCP)** and **Internet Protocol (IP)**, or TCP/IP, the standard protocol suite for the internet.

- 1983 – Scientists created top-level domains for the **Domain Name System (DNS)**, such as .edu, .com, and .gov.

While there were a few reports of viruses making their way through computer systems, most anyone who worked with or knew about the internet never thought anything malicious could happen. That was until 1988, when *Robert Morris*, a *Cornell University* student, wrote and released a worm.

> **Important note**
> A worm is a self-propagating virus that can spread on its own.

The worm, later dubbed the *Morris worm*, created a crippling effect on the fledgling internet. As a result, Robert Morris was tried and convicted under the *1986 Computer Fraud and Abuse Act*. Soon afterward, the idea of cybersecurity began to take hold. And more specifically, it became more apparent that our data could be at risk.

Over the next three decades, many more threats emerged, such as social engineering, malware, and denial of service attacks:

- **Social engineering**: This is a combination of methods designed to fraudulently obtain information about an organization or computer system. Effective social engineering techniques rely on the malicious actor's ability to con someone into providing information, by using social skills and powers of influence.

- **Malware**: This is malicious software that includes viruses, rootkits, spyware, and trojans. Most malware is designed to infiltrate a computer system or network to gain unauthorized access to critical information. Other forms of malware, such as ransomware, are designed to lock a system and its resources until someone pays a ransom.

- **Denial of Service (DoS)**: These attacks will send numerous requests to a system in an effort to interrupt or suspend services to legitimate users. In most cases, the malicious actor(s) will use a **Distributed Denial of Service (DDoS)** attack, which is more effective as it uses armies or botnets to launch an attack.

As outlined, there are many different types of data, such as images, documents, and video. Data can be a part of an organization, such as a business or government entity, or belong to an individual. Let's compare the two next.

Categorizing data

Data can represent either an individual's information or details that relate to a business or organization.

An individual's private data is generally referred to as **Personally Identifiable Information (PII)**, which is information that can be used to identify someone. PII can include bank account records, social security numbers, or credit card information.

Proprietary business data includes information that if exposed can result in harm to the organization. Protected business data includes financial data, earnings reports, employee records, and trade secrets.

On any network, there are several goals or services we strive to provide, such as confidentiality, integrity, and availability. Let's explore this concept in the next section.

Understanding security services

Today, there are many threats to the security of our data. Therefore, it's imperative that we remain vigilant in protecting our networks and data from attack or unauthorized access. In this section, we'll take a look at some of the security services designed to assure our data is protected. We'll also see how cryptographic techniques can help ensure data is not modified, lost, or accessed in an unauthorized manner.

There are many guidelines that outline how to provide data security. One document that helps list security concepts is the **International Telecommunications Union (ITU)** *Security architecture for Open Systems Interconnection for CCITT applications*, also known as **X.800**. Let's take a look.

Investigating X.800

The **Consultative Committee for International Telephony and Telegraphy (CCITT)**, now known as the **International Telecommunications Union - Telecommunication Standardization Sector (ITU-T)**, recognized the need to provide a secure architecture when dealing with data transmission. More specifically, they wanted to outline the general framework of security services that should be implemented within the **Open Systems Interconnection (OSI)** model.

> **Important note**
> The OSI model is a seven-layer representation of how systems communicate with one another. The OSI model is well recognized among network professionals, as it breaks down the function of each layer.

X.800 outlines recommended security services, along with best-practice logical and physical controls that help protect each service. In addition to logical and physical controls, the document outlines various cryptographic techniques that should be used, such as the following:

- **Encryption**: Transforms plaintext into ciphertext by using a cryptographic algorithm and key.
- **Hashing**: Functions that take a given input (of any size) and produce a fixed-length output. The output size will depend on the algorithm. This is also called a one-way function, in that you cannot derive the original input from the hash value.

- **Digital signature**: A cryptographic technique using asymmetric encryption to ensure message authenticity and non-repudiation.

The document lists the main security services designed to protect data, which include confidentiality, integrity, authentication, and non-repudiation.

Let's take a look at each of these and how they can be achieved, starting with confidentiality.

Ensuring confidentiality

While we may not feel that all data should be rigorously protected, in today's world, it's best to keep most, if not all, data protected from prying eyes. Confidentiality means keeping private data private by protecting against unauthorized disclosure.

An example of a violation of confidentiality would be if a malicious actor were to gain access to a company's proprietary trade secrets or customer database.

A data breach of client information can cause business harm and result in a tarnished reputation and loss of trust. To ensure confidentiality, businesses and individuals should restrict access by using access control methods that allow only authorized people, devices, or processes to have access to the data.

In addition, we can protect data confidentiality by using encryption. That way, if someone were to gain access to the information, it would be meaningless, unless they have a key to decrypt the data.

Another service is to ensure data integrity, as we'll see next.

Safeguarding integrity

Providing integrity ensures that data is not modified, lost, or destroyed in either an accidental or unauthorized manner.

An example of a violation of integrity would be someone gaining access to their payroll file and changing their salary from $30,000 to $40,000.

To protect integrity, use access control methods and employ strong audit policies. In addition, monitor the network for unusual or suspicious activity and use software designed to compare cryptographic hash values for unauthorized changes to the data.

One example of software that monitors for unauthorized changes in the filesystem is called *Tripwire*, which acts as a software *intrusion detection* system.

Tripwire works in the following manner:

1. Prior to activating the monitoring feature, you must first flag the files that need to be checked on all filesystems and devices.

2. Once the appropriate files are identified, the software will baseline the existing filesystem and generate a hash value for all files.

3. After baselining, the software will scan the filesystem and generate another hash value for all flagged files.

4. The software then compares each file's hash value against the baseline.

5. If the hash value does not match the baseline, the system will send an alert, which will indicate that the file has been modified in an unauthorized manner.

In the following figure, the hash value of the baseline file is not the same as the hash value of the checked file:

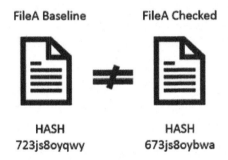

Figure 1.2 – A hash value that does not match the baseline

If the hash value does not match, this will send an alert that there is a violation of the integrity of the file.

Another service that is paramount on a network is authentication, as we'll see next.

Providing authentication

When something or someone is authentic, we are assured that it is true or genuine. For example, when you go to a bank to cash a check, the bank will require you to produce identification to prove who you are.

A violation of authentication occurs when spoofing techniques are used. For example, malicious actors often use an email address that spoofs the name to look like someone you know. This is a social engineering technique that is used to get you to open a file or complete some action.

When dealing with an entity on a network, it's especially important to guarantee authenticity, as this assures both parties that the message has originated from an authorized source. One way to prove authentication is by using a message authentication code, which is a small block of code used to authenticate the origin of the message.

Another security service is non-repudiation, which prevents an entity from denying that they either sent or received a communication.

Certifying non-repudiation

Non-repudiation is preventing a party from denying participation in a communication and can be used in both sides of a conversation to prevent either party from denying their involvement. By using a digital signature, non-repudiation can be achieved in the following manner:

- **Proof of origin**: Assurance that the message was *sent* by a specific entity
- **Proof of receipt**: Assurance that the message was *received* by a specific entity

To understand the importance of providing non-repudiation, let's outline the concept using a scenario in the following section.

Denying involvement

Every day, busy professionals send and receive emails. So that you can better understand how this works, I'll outline the concept in a story where using a digital signature when sending an email could help provide non-repudiation.

Bob is an office manager for a large payroll department. The supervisor is Jessica, who oversees the day-to-day operations of the department. Jessica is generally busy, with many tasks and meetings throughout the day.

Jessica's administrative assistant, Paul, notices that Jessica's birthday is in 2 days. Paul emails Bob to purchase a birthday cake and plan a surprise party and invite the whole office. Bob completes all the necessary arrangements and lets Paul and the department know that everything is ready for Friday.

On Friday, Jessica returns from her morning meeting, where she is greeted by the entire department wishing her a happy birthday. Jessica looks around the room and is visibly upset, and states, "you shouldn't have done this." She then retreats to her office and closes the door.

Later that morning, Jessica calls Bob and Paul into her office and tells them that she knows they meant well, but she didn't appreciate the attention. Paul states that he has no idea how this happened. Bob replies to Paul, "you sent me an email telling me to plan the event!" Paul answers, "no I didn't."

At that point, Bob has no recourse but to take the blame, as Paul has repudiated the fact that he had requested the party.

While Bob could have printed the email from Paul to attempt to prove that Paul requested the party, this may not be sufficient, as it is possible to spoof (or recreate) an email. However, if Paul had sent the email using a digital signature, this would prove that he had sent the email. At that point, Bob could have defended himself and let Jessica know what really happened.

Using a digital signature to prevent non-repudiation is not always required; however, in a high-stakes situation, such as a financial transaction, this can be especially important.

On any network, it's also important to ensure availability, as we'll see next.

Assuring availability

Availability is the assurance that resources are available to authorized devices, users, and/ or processes on the network.

A violation of availability would be a DoS attack designed to interrupt or suspend services to legitimate users.

Although ensuring availability is an important concept, we cannot use a cryptographic method to ensure this service. However, there are other ways to protect availability, such as using intrusion detection and prevention. In addition, the network administrator should also keep systems up to date with all security patches, and upgrade systems and devices when necessary.

As outlined, encryption and cryptographic techniques are some of the ways through which we can protect against the constant threats to the security of our data. In the next section, let's take a look at a few of the cryptographic concepts that you might encounter.

Introducing common cryptographic concepts

In order to securely exchange data, we use more than just encryption algorithms. We also use several cryptographic tools and techniques. When discussing these concepts, you will hear terms such as **symmetric** and **asymmetric encryption**, along with **cryptographic hash**.

> **Important note**
> You will get a better understanding of these terms as we progress through the chapters. If you need a quick review, visit `https://www.makeuseof.com/tag/encryption-terms/` for an explanation of 11 of the most common encryption terms.

In this section, we'll provide the broad strokes of the concepts of a TTP and the PKI to help your understanding. In addition, since you'll often see an explanation of a complex topic using the names of fictional characters, we'll talk about the story of Bob and Alice.

We'll go into the details of the aforementioned terms and others as the book progresses. For now, let's start with the importance of a TTP.

Trusting a TTP

Think about doing a transaction on the internet. When you go to an online shopping site, you will want to encrypt your transactions to provide confidentiality as you exchange data with the website. Let's consider the following scenario.

Alice wants to purchase some pet supplies for her two cats. She heads out to the pet supply store, *Kiddikatz*. If the communication is not encrypted, the transaction could be intercepted and read by Mallory, a malicious active attacker, as part of a **Man-in-The-Middle (MiTM)** attack, as shown in the following graphic:

| Alice | Mallory | Kiddikatz |

Figure 1.3 – A MiTM attack

To prevent a MiTM attack, Alice will use **Transport Layer Security (TLS)** to encrypt and secure the transaction. Prior to the transaction, both parties will need to exchange keys. That is where the TTP becomes important.

A TTP is necessary in a hybrid cryptosystem. In a faceless, nameless environment such as the internet, TTPs helps us to communicate securely on the web.

The idea of a TTP works by using transitive trust. As shown in the following graphic, we see that if Alice trusts the TTP, and Kiddikatz trusts the TTP, then Alice automatically trusts Kiddikatz:

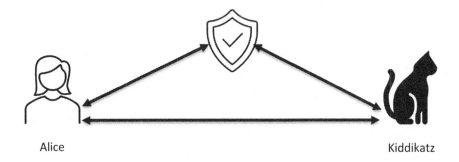

Figure 1.4 – A transaction using a TTP

We know that TTPs are important in a digital transaction. Next, let's see how you can determine whether or not a site can be trusted.

Ensuring trust on the network

When you go to your browser and you see a lock next to the web address, that means you can trust the site. As shown in the following screenshot, we can see that the site for *Packt Publishing* is a secure connection:

Figure 1.5 – Secure website for Packt Publishing

Some companies that provide this trust include Verisign, Cloudflare, Google Trust Services, and Thawte. All of this is made possible because of the PKI, as outlined next.

Managing keys using the PKI

As we have seen, a TTP provides the trust required when completing transactions on the internet. During a transaction, all entities are able to securely communicate with one another by using the PKI.

Although the term Public Key Infrastructure implies that the PKI generates keys, that is not the case. Instead, the PKI generates a digital certificate to securely distribute keys between a server (such as a web server) and a client. PKI uses a TTP to generate a certificate, which provides the authentication for each entity.

Let's step through the process of distributing public keys by using a certificate.

Obtaining the certificates

Encryption algorithms use keys. There are two main types of encryption. The type of encryption will determine whether one or two keys are used. The difference is as follows:

- **Symmetric encryption**: Uses a single shared key (or secret) key
- **Asymmetric encryption**: Uses a pair of keys – a public key and a private key

When using asymmetric encryption, an entity's private key is kept private. However, the public key is shared for everyone to see, as it is public.

When obtaining someone's public key for a transaction, we need to be able to trust that the key is from the entity from whom we received it. As a result, when completing transactions on the internet, we use a TTP.

As shown in the following diagram, the TTP provides a certificate to each entity, which ensures proof of identity and holds the other party's verified public key:

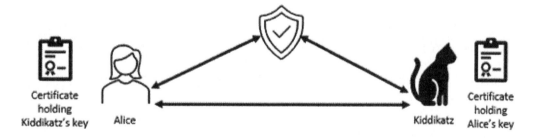

Certificate holding Kiddikatz's key   Alice

Kiddikatz   Certificate holding Alice's key

Figure 1.6 – Certificate exchange in the PKI

The PKI provides the structure necessary to ensure trust and securely share the public keys between those involved in a digital transaction.

Once Alice and Kiddikatz are assured trust in one another, they can securely exchange the session key and begin the transaction.

When discussing cryptography, it is common to use themes, much like the ones used in programming, such as *Foo Bar* and *Hello World*. In the next section, let's get to know the story of Bob, Alice, and other characters, which will help us when explaining cryptographic concepts.

Getting to know Bob and Alice

When outlining technical concepts, it's important to provide an easy-to-understand explanation. Using a story with characters helps explain technical topics.

Using the characters *Alice* and *Bob* is the most common way we use to explain cryptographic concepts. For example, you might see the following when describing a scenario:

Alice needs to send Bob a secure message. They must first obtain the same shared key.

If you need more characters, there are others you can use. The characters are listed in *Bruce Schneier's* book *Applied Cryptography*, where he presents a list of characters that include the following:

- **Alice**: Primary participant in the transaction
- **Bob**: Secondary participant in the transaction
- **Mallory**: A malicious (MiTM) attacker
- **Eve**: An eavesdropper, usually a passive attacker
- **Victor** or **Vanna**: A verifier
- **Trent**: A TTP

Using the names of individuals makes complex concepts more relatable. As a result, we will see more of Bob and Alice throughout our discussion on cryptography.

When discussing encryption, one of the simplest ways to conceal the true meaning of data is by using substitution and transposition, as we'll see next.

Outlining substitution and transposition

We can define cryptography as hidden or secret writing. The concept of concealing information using secret codes began thousands of years ago. Some of the early methods to encrypt data used pen, paper, or even rings, such as the *pigpen*, or *Freemason*, cipher.

In this section, we'll take a look at early encryption techniques, called classic cryptography, which mainly used transposition and substitution. The two work in the following manner:

- Transposition ciphers *transpose* letters according to a pattern.

- Substitution ciphers *substitute* each letter with a different letter according to the key.

In addition, we'll also take a look at methods to break the encryption. Let's start with seeing how substitution works, along with an example using the pigpen cipher.

Substituting characters

Substitution techniques to encode text work by substituting one character for another. The characters can be letters, numbers, or special characters. There are several substitution ciphers. One example is the *pigpen* or *Freemason* cipher. This cipher uses a grid formation with symbols that represent the different letters, as shown in the following figure:

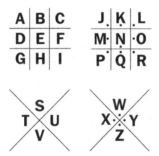

Figure 1.7 – Pigpen cipher code

To generate a code, you would substitute each letter with the corresponding symbol. For example, the phrase *Secret message* converted using a pigpen cipher would appear as the following code:

Figure 1.8 – The phrase "Secret message" converted to code using a pigpen cipher

Try this yourself by going to https://www.boxentriq.com/code-breaking/pigpen-cipher.

Another technique to scramble data is by using transposition, as we'll see next.

Transposing the text

There are several techniques to transpose text. Unlike substitution, which substitutes one character for another, transposition transposes or rearranges the characters according to a pattern.

One method to transpose characters is reversing the order of letters in a phrase. The phrase *confidentiality is keeping private data private* will become *etavirp atad etavirp gnipeek si ytilaitnedifnoc.*

Even though this is a simple transposition of characters, you might have difficulty determining what the phrase means, unless you know that the letters have been reversed.

The *rail fence*, or *zig-zag*, cipher is another transposition cipher that conceals data by using *rails* or separate lines of text.

For example, if we were to transpose the word *TRANSPOSE* by using three rails and filling in the blank spaces using other letters, we would have the following output:

T	Y	I	N	S	U	P	C	E
K	R	I	N	M	P	U	S	U
K	Y	A	W	Q	Z	O	A	B

Figure 1.9 – The rail fence cipher concealing text

If someone were to look at the three lines of text, they may not be able to determine the meaning, unless they know the pattern, as shown:

T	Y	I	N	S	U	P	C	E
K	R	I	N	M	P	U	S	U
K	Y	A	W	Q	Z	O	A	B

Figure 1.10 – The rail fence cipher with the text exposed

Both the substitution and transposition ciphers are simple ciphers where it is fairly easy to break the code to determine the plaintext. When working with methods to conceal text such as substitution and transposition, we can use various methods to break the code, as outlined next.

Breaking the code

Concurrent to creating ways to conceal data using basic cryptographic techniques came the need to break codes and ciphers by using various methods.

With classic cryptography, code-breaking is a lot like a word puzzle, where the key is found by substituting letters until you determine a match. Because some methods use transposition, you might need to evaluate the text for alternate patterns that rearrange the text in some way.

Ciphers that use one alphabet are called *mono-alphabetic* ciphers. If only one alphabet is used, we can employ letter frequency analysis, as described next.

Analyzing the frequency of the letters

Letter frequency analysis is a cryptographic tool. The analysis begins by determining the frequency of the letters so that the actual message can be found.

When using letter frequency analysis, English characters can be divided into groups that include the following:

- The high-frequency group includes letters such as A, E, and T.
- The low-frequency or rare group includes letters such as K, Q, X, and Z.
- *Digrams* are pairs of letters that include th, he, of, and it. You'll also want to consider pairs using repeating letters such as ll, oo, or ee.
- *Trigrams* are collections of three letters that include the, est, and, for, and his.

To adequately produce a frequency profile, you need a generous amount of characters. You can manually count the characters or use one of the applications available online, such as the one found at `http://www.richkni.co.uk/php/crypta/freq.php`.

If the cipher uses more than one alphabet, this will make the code more difficult to decrypt. You might even find text that doesn't use an alphabet. For example, try to decode the following message:

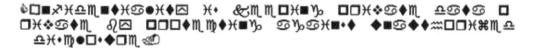

Figure 1.11 – Secret code

You can find the answer at the end of this chapter under the *Assessments* section.

As we can see, even simple cryptographic methods can conceal information from someone. The downside is the simpler the method, the easier it is to obtain the plaintext message.

Summary

Every day, more and more services are being added to our infrastructures, homes, and businesses, making network security a constant challenge. However, a secure network is important as it protects the organization. In this chapter, we took a look at the threats to our data that exist, which makes securely managing a large volume of data in various locations a challenge. We saw the importance of providing security services such as confidentiality, integrity, and availability, and how using cryptographic techniques can help protect those services.

We then took a look at some common cryptographic concepts, such as TTPs and key management using the PKI. We also got to know characters such as Bob, Alice, Trent, and Mallory, which help us to personalize and better understand complex cryptographic concepts. Finally, we took a look at two basic cryptographic concepts, substitution, and transposition. We saw how substitution substitutes plaintext characters with other characters to convert it into ciphertext. We also learned how transposition rearranges the characters of plaintext to conceal information. We then saw how we can use letter frequency analysis to crack a simple code, that uses a monoalphabetic cipher.

So that you can better understand the evolution of encryption, the next chapter will start with a review of some classical ciphers such as the *Vigenère* and *Caesar* ciphers. Then we'll examine how war efforts prompted the encoding of transmissions, and how the *Enigma* was used to securely send messages. We'll then learn the beginnings of the **Data Encryption Standard** (**DES**), with the development of *Lucifer* and *Feistel* ciphers, as scientists recognized the need to secure digital data.

Questions

Now it's time to check your knowledge. Select the best response, then check your answers with those found in the *Assessment* section at the end of the book.

1. In _____, Ray Tomlinson created electronic mail (email).

    a. 1968

    b. 1972

    c. 1992

    d. 1998

2. When protecting data, _____ ensures that data is not modified, lost, or destroyed in either an accidental or unauthorized manner.

   a. integrity

   b. confidentiality

   c. availability

   d. authentication

3. A digital _____ is a cryptographic technique using asymmetric encryption that ensures a message is authentic and has not been modified or altered while in transit.

   a. breadcrumb

   b. cookie

   c. rail fence

   d. signature

4. When malicious actors often use an email address that spoofs the name to look like someone you know, this is a violation of _____.

   a. integrity

   b. confidentiality

   c. availability

   d. authentication

5. _____ encryption uses a pair of keys: a public key and a private key.

   a. Verified

   b. Asymmetric

   c. Symmetric

   d. SHA-1

6. _____ ciphers substitute each letter with a different letter according to the key.

   a. Allocation

   b. Substitution

   c. Transposition

   d. Pigpen

7. The rail fence, or zig-zag, cipher is a _____ cipher that conceals data by using "rails" or separate lines of text.

    a. allocation

    b. substitution

    c. transposition

    d. pigpen

Further reading

Please refer to the following links for more information:

- Take a stroll down memory lane and visit some of the most significant events in computer history by going to `https://www.computerhistory.org`.

- For a comparison on prices of hard drives per GB, visit `https://mkomo.com/cost-per-gigabyte`.

- To help you understand how much data is in a petabyte, exabyte, zettabyte, or yottabyte, go to `http://highscalability.com/blog/2012/9/11/how-big-is-a-petabyte-exabyte-zettabyte-or-a-yottabyte.html`.

- To review some of the topics related to internet security, take a look at the internet glossary found at `https://tools.ietf.org/html/rfc2828`.

- To learn more about Bob and Alice and related topics, go to `http://cryptocouple.com/`.

- The X.800 document is found at `https://www.itu.int/rec/T-REC-X.800-199103-I/en`. Go to the middle of the page and select the PDF format. Once in the document, you will see that it was drafted in 1991. However, it still remains applicable.

- To get a better understanding of transposition ciphers along with some examples, visit `https://crypto.interactive-maths.com/simple-transposition-ciphers.html`.

- You can read more on Tripwire at `https://www.tripwire.com/`.

2
The Evolution of Ciphers

Over the last several centuries, we have seen advancements in civilization, along with improvements in technology. As a result, we have seen an evolution in the methods used to conceal information. To set the foundation for more advanced topics that we will be covering in this book, we'll review some ancient techniques to conceal information. We'll start with a brief overview of some early ways to hide messages. We'll learn how data was concealed using a tool called a scytale, along with a radical method using a tattoo etched on a trusted servant's head. We'll then see how data was concealed using monoalphabetic and then polyalphabetic ciphers along with an example of each, using both the Caesar and Vigenère ciphers.

We'll then see how the effect of war led to advances in the way to encode and securely transmit messages. We'll discover how Claude Shannon, whose early research is still influential in modern-day encryption, outlined the concepts of using substitution and permutation to encode data more effectively. Finally, we'll see how with the advent of computerization in the 1960s and 1970s, the need to protect digital data became increasingly evident. As a result, we'll see the development of the Feistel cipher, a precursor to the **Data Encryption Standard** (**DES**) that is used to secure digital data.

In this chapter, we're going to cover the following main topics:

- Early uses of cryptography

- Encoding transmissions during war

- Entering the digital age

Early uses of cryptography

For thousands of years, we have been trying to conceal private information in a variety of ways. Today, we use cryptographic techniques to protect credit card information, **personally identifiable information** (**PII**), and online transactions. However, over the years, much of the effort to protect information has stemmed from activity surrounding war efforts. Concealing information was done in an attempt to prevent the enemy from gaining access to sensitive information.

In this section, we'll take a look at some ancient ways to hide messages. We'll start with a few of the early examples used, which includes the scytale and even tattoos. We'll also review monoalphabetic ciphers, such as the Caesar cipher. We'll then review the introduction of polyalphabetic ciphers, using the Vigenère cipher as an example.

Let's start with a brief look at some ancient ways to conceal information.

Using tattoos and scytales

Early iterations of obscuring information involved using symbols, such as hieroglyphics, during the time period around 1900 **Before Common Era** (**BCE**) by the Egyptians.

As shown in the following figure, there were several different types of symbols used:

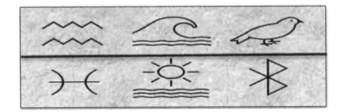

Figure 2.1 – Hieroglyphic images

However, the meaning is unclear unless you understand what the symbols represent. While hieroglyphics may not have been intentionally vague, the concept relates to modern-day cryptography, in that the message won't mean anything unless you have a key to decode the information.

A lesser-known method involves tattooing a message on the head, as we'll see next.

Tattooing a message

What better way to conceal information than by hiding in plain sight? That is the basis of the approach used to send a message from one Greek ruler to another during the 6th century BCE.

The Greek leader *Histiaeus*, son of *Lysagoras*, wanted to launch an uprising against the king of Persia, *Darius I*. In order to get a message to another Greek ruler to launch a revolt against *Darius I*, *Histiaeus* devised a plan using his most trusted servant.

Histiaeus shaved the servant's scalp, tattooed a simple message on his head, and then waited for the servant's hair to grow back. Once the message was concealed by hair, *Histiaeus* sent the servant to an ally, *Aristagoras*, the leader of the *Ionian Greeks*. The servant told *Aristagoras* that he had a message from *Histiaeus* and explained that in order to see the message, *Aristagoras* had to shave his head. *Aristagoras* then shaved the servant's head, which revealed the message *REVOLT*.

This early example of concealing a message illustrates how, even centuries ago, we had a need to keep information confidential. Another example of an innovative way to hide information is by using a scytale. Let's take a look.

Wrapping parchment

The Greeks and the Spartans around the time of the 7th century BCE also devised a method to secretly communicate. The method used a carefully constructed block of wood, and a thin strip of parchment with lettering on the parchment.

The tool, called a scytale, was one of the first methods to encode text, and is considered a transposition cipher, as it transposes the letters. Both the sender and receiver had the same tool to encrypt and decrypt the secret message.

To create the message, the sender would need to do the following:

1. Wrap the parchment around the scytale.
2. Write the message across one line.
3. Fill in the rest of the lines with random characters.

To read the message, the receiver would need to do the following:

1. Wrap the parchment around the scytale.
2. Read the message.

As shown in the following figure, once the thin strip of parchment was wrapped around the block of wood, the message would then appear:

Figure 2.2 – A scytale

The message meant nothing without the scytale, as it just looked like a strip of parchment with some lettering, as shown in the following figure:

Figure 2.3 – Message on parchment

Although simple by today's standards, during that time period, the scytale was an effective way to covertly send messages.

Many of the early ways to conceal messages involved using a single alphabet. Later on, methods to use more than one alphabet to further obscure the message were developed. Let's explore the concept of monoalphabetic and polyalphabetic substitution ciphers next.

Evaluating monoalphabetic ciphers

A monoalphabetic substitution cipher uses a single alphabet and substitutes one letter or character for another. Characters can include letters, special characters such as an exclamation point or a pound sign, along with punctuation marks. This basic cipher uses a key to decode the message.

An example of a monoalphabetic substitution cipher is the Caesar, or shift, cipher. Let's see an example next.

Examining the Caesar cipher

The Caesar cipher was created by Julius Caesar so that he could keep certain information confidential. This simple cipher shifts the letters over by a predetermined number of spaces to encode the message.

For example, if we shift over by two spaces, A will become F, and B will become G, and so on, as shown in the following diagram:

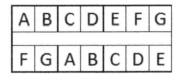

Figure 2.4 – Caesar shift over by two

In some, but not all, cases, the letters are wrapped around. To decode the message, you need to shift each letter back by the predetermined number of spaces.

The cipher was developed in around 50 BCE and was effective, in that you could not decode the message unless you knew the shift amount. Another reason the cipher was effective was that, during that time, scholars felt that only about 10-20% of the population could read and write. As a result, even if someone were to be able to determine the shift, they might not be able to read the message, which provided another level of security.

A monoalphabetic substitution cipher is a simple cipher that can be cracked by using letter frequency analysis. As time passed, stronger ciphers were developed. That included the use of more than one alphabet, as we'll discuss next.

Recognizing polyalphabetic ciphers

In 1563, Giovanni Battista Porta published the book *De furtivis literarum notis*, or *The Secret of Letters*, which outlined the use of various ciphers. Porta developed the Porta Cipher, which is a polyalphabetic substitution cipher.

A polyalphabetic cipher uses more than one alphabet to encode text. The additional alphabet is resistant to the use of letter frequency analysis and provides an additional layer of confusion when attempting to decode the message.

Another example of a polyalphabetic cipher is the Vigenère cipher. Let's take a look.

Studying the Vigenère cipher

In 1586, Blaise de Vigenère developed a polyalphabetic substitution cipher that used a table that had two alphabets. The two alphabets are arranged in a table, as shown in the following figure:

```
  A B C D E F G H I J K L M N O P Q R S T Y V W X Y Z
A A B C D E F G H I J K L M N O P Q R S T Y V W X Y Z
B B C D E F G H I J K L M N O P Q R S T Y V W X Y Z A
C C D E F G H I J K L M N O P Q R S T Y V W X Y Z A C
D D E F G H I J K L M N O P Q R S T Y V W X Y Z A B C
E E F G H I J K L M N O P Q R S T Y V W X Y Z A B C D
F F G H I J K L M N O P Q R S T Y V W X Y Z A B C D E
G G H I J K L M N O P Q R S T Y V W X Y Z A B C D E F
H H I J K L M N O P Q R S T Y V W X Y Z A B C D E F G
I I J K L M N O P Q R S T Y V W X Y Z A B C D E F G H
J J K L M N O P Q R S T Y V W X Y Z A B C D E F G H I
K K L M N O P Q R S T Y V W X Y Z A B C D E F G H I J
L L M N O P Q R S T Y V W X Y Z A B C D E F G H I J K
M M N O P Q R S T Y V W X Y Z A B C D E F G H I J K L
N N O P Q R S T Y V W X Y Z A B C D E F G H I J K L M
O O P Q R S T Y V W X Y Z A B C D E F G H I J K L M N
P P Q R S T Y V W X Y Z A B C D E F G H I J K L M N O
Q Q R S T Y V W X Y Z A B C D E F G H I J K L M N O P
R R S T Y V W X Y Z A B C D E F G H I J K L M N O P Q
S S T Y V W X Y Z A B C D E F G H I J K L M N O P Q R
T T Y V W X Y Z A B C D E F G H I J K L M N O P Q R S
Y Y V W X Y Z A B C D E F G H I J K L M N O P Q R S T
V V W X Y Z A B C D E F G H I J K L M N O P Q R S T Y
W W X Y Z A B C D E F G H I J K L M N O P Q R S T Y V
X X Y Z A B C D E F G H I J K L M N O P Q R S T Y V W
Y Y Z A B C D E F G H I J K L M N O P Q R S T Y V W X
Z Z A B C D E F G H I J K L M N O P Q R S T Y V W X Y
```

Figure 2.5 – The Vigenère square

The letters are arranged in a pattern using a right circular shift in each row. Once the row is shifted, the character at the end is moved to the first position. The first row does not shift; the remaining rows shift as follows:

- The second row shifts to the right by one.

- The third row shifts to the right by two.

The shifts continue until the last row, which shifts to the right by 25, and the character at the end is moved to the first position.

Text is encoded by the intersection of a key (or secret word) and the message. For example, we will use the following:

- The phrase is LET'S STUDY CRYPTOGRAPHY.

- The key, or secret word, is TIGERKITTENS.

To encode the text, we will remove any apostrophes or spaces and put the phrase LET'S STUDY CRYPTOGRAPHY along the top. Below, we will put the secret phrase, TIGERKITTENS, which will repeat until the end of the characters as follows:

L	E	T	S	S	T	U	D	Y	C	R	Y	P	T	O	G	R	A	P	H	Y
T	I	G	E	R	K	I	T	T	E	N	S	T	I	G	E	R	K	I	T	T

Figure 2.6 Table with phrase and secret word

Using the table, we will take the first letter, L, which will intersect with the first letter of the secret word, T, which results in the letter E, as shown in the following figure:

```
  A B C D E F G H I J K L M N O P Q R S T Y V W X Y Z
A A B C D E F G H I J K L M N O P Q R S T Y V W X Y Z
B B C D E F G H I J K L M N O P Q R S T Y V W X Y Z A
C C D E F G H I J K L M N O P Q R S T Y V W X Y Z A C
D D E F G H I J K L M N O P Q R S T Y V W X Y Z A B C
E E F G H I J K L M N O P Q R S T Y V W X Y Z A B C D
F F G H I J K L M N O P Q R S T Y V W X Y Z A B C D E
G G H I J K L M N O P Q R S T Y V W X Y Z A B C D E F
H H I J K L M N O P Q R S T Y V W X Y Z A B C D E F G
I I J K L M N O P Q R S T Y V W X Y Z A B C D E F G H
J J K L M N O P Q R S T Y V W X Y Z A B C D E F G H I
K K L M N O P Q R S T Y V W X Y Z A B C D E F G H I J
L L M N O P Q R S T Y V W X Y Z A B C D E F G H I J K
M M N O P Q R S T Y V W X Y Z A B C D E F G H I J K L
N N O P Q R S T Y V W X Y Z A B C D E F G H I J K L M
O O P Q R S T Y V W X Y Z A B C D E F G H I J K L M N
P P Q R S T Y V W X Y Z A B C D E F G H I J K L M N O
Q Q R S T Y V W X Y Z A B C D E F G H I J K L M N O P
R R S T Y V W X Y Z A B C D E F G H I J K L M N O P Q
S S T Y V W X Y Z A B C D E F G H I J K L M N O P Q R
T T Y V W X Y Z A B C D[E]F G H I J K L M N O P Q R S
Y Y V W X Y Z A B C D E F G H I J K L M N O P Q R S T
V V W X Y Z A B C D E F G H I J K L M N O P Q R S T Y
W W X Y Z A B C D E F G H I J K L M N O P Q R S T Y V
X X Y Z A B C D E F G H I J K L M N O P Q R S T Y V W
Y Y Z A B C D E F G H I J K L M N O P Q R S T Y V W X
Z Z A B C D E F G H I J K L M N O P Q R S T Y V W X Y
```

Figure 2.7 – The first letter of the phrase intersecting with the first letter of the secret word

We'll then take the second letter, E, which intersects with the second letter of the secret word, I, and results in the letter M. All letters are evaluated to produce the output, as shown in the last row of the following table:

L	E	T	S	S	T	U	D	Y	C	R	Y	P	T	O	G	R	A	P	H	Y
T	I	G	E	R	K	I	T	T	E	N	S	T	I	G	E	R	K	I	T	T
E	M	Z	W	J	D	C	W	R	G	E	Q	I	B	U	K	I	K	X	A	R

Figure 2.8 – Table with phrase after encrypting text

As you can see, the message would be difficult to decode without the key.

Throughout history, much of the need to conceal messages was during a time of conflict or war, as we'll see next.

Encoding transmissions during war

A primary driver to conceal information from prying eyes is war, mainly because, during a conflict such as a war, it's critical to communicate with allies to transmit information about the enemy, along with reports and attack plans. During any conflict, whether on land, air, or at sea, encoding the message is key in preventing information from being intercepted by the enemy.

In this section, we'll take a brief look at communication methods over the years. We'll then take a closer look at the Enigma machine, a complex German engineered device used in World War II that created strong encrypted messages.

Let's start with a discussion on communication methods that are essential during battle.

Communicating during wartime

During a war, the ability to communicate offers military leaders the advantage to control, coordinate, and oversee their armies. If a military leader is unable to effectively communicate with their allies, this could lead to a crushing defeat.

Throughout the years, communication techniques have been developed and improved, all with the goal of being able to provide split-second communication to the troops. Methods have varied according to the technology and the location of the signal.

Whether on land, sea, or air, communication methods could have included any of the following:

- Primitive methods such as riders on horseback and bicycles, homing pigeons, and messenger dogs

- Visual techniques such as sail movements, signal flags, cannon blasts, and coordinated lighting techniques

- More sophisticated approaches, such as telegraphs, radio, and telephones

Let's take a look at some of the more sophisticated techniques used. We'll start with a discussion on Morse code, which uses electrical pulses, along with flash signaling, which used lights to transmit information.

Using Morse code and flash signaling

In the years before the American Civil War, Samuel F.B. Morse developed a technique that sent electrical signals over copper wire. Called Morse code, the signaling worked in the following manner:

- Three dots equal a dash.

- Spaces within a letter equal one dot.

- Spacing between letters equals three dots.

- Spacing between two words equals seven dots.

For example, the first three letters of the alphabet use dashes and dots as follows:

Figure 2.9 – The letters A, B, and C represented in Morse code

Morse code changed the landscape for war efforts such as the American Civil War, as it enabled speedy signal communication. To hear what Morse code sounds like, visit https://www.youtube.com/watch?v=_J8YcQETyTw.

Another related technique was flash signaling, which generated signals using long and short flashes of light. An example of a device used to transmit light was a heliograph, which had two mirrors that captured sunlight, and allowed the operator to transmit Morse-code-like signals. The heliograph had limited use, in that it required sunlight to transmit the signal.

Later on, during the last half of the 19th century, came more advanced technologies that enhanced the ability to communicate, such as the telephone and radio. Let's explore these concepts.

Transmitting via phone and radio

The telephone was invented by Alexander Graham Bell in 1876. However, the telephone was not universally available to everyone until years later. The phone technology evolved, expanded, and slowly became available to more individuals from the late 1800s into the early 1900s.

Military leaders saw the value of using the telephone during wartime. Phone lines were either strung using telephone poles or buried in trenches, which allowed the ability to keep in touch with the troops during conflict.

Although an invaluable tool, there was always the threat of someone cutting the phone lines, or the lines being destroyed by artillery fire, which then severed the ability to communicate.

Near the end of the 1800s, another powerful communication method, the radio, was developed and used wireless signals instead of electrical pulses. Also called the wireless telegraph, this enhanced the ability to communicate information using radio waves, with no danger of someone cutting the wires. However, radio signals introduced a new threat, which was the ability of someone to intercept the signal.

Although in its infancy, radio was used early in the 1900s to aid in communicating during World War I. By World War II, radio use had expanded and evolved. The devices became more powerful, portable, and had the ability to transmit communications over greater ranges.

As the war progressed, the need to transmit securely became more evident. With the threat of someone eavesdropping on the signal came the need to come up with creative ways to secure the transmissions.

One significant device developed to encrypt data transmissions during the war was the Enigma machine, as we'll learn next.

Examining the Enigma machine

Along with the ability to transmit via radio came the threat of someone intercepting the signals. As a result, the need to conceal or encrypt messages to keep information from the enemy became paramount.

Shortly after the end of WWI, a German engineer, Arthur Scherbius, developed a mechanical device that was capable of creating strong coded messages that were nearly impossible to crack. The device, called the Enigma, had four main components, as follows:

- Five rotors, of which the operator would use three at a time; the rotors could be adjusted (or rotated) according to the desired settings

- A keyboard with 26 keys that corresponded to the letters of the alphabet and was streamlined, in that you couldn't enter any spaces, special characters, numbers, or returns

- The lampboard, which was illuminated when a letter was encoded

- A plugboard or tiny switchboard (also called the steckers)

A representation of the Enigma is shown in the following diagram, with an approximation of each of the components:

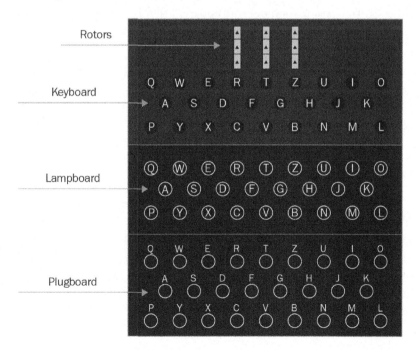

Figure 2.10 – The Enigma machine

To further encode the text, the operator could use the plugboard (or steckers), which had 26 sockets. By using a wire with two jacks, the operator would insert one end into a plug (or letter), and the other jack into another plug (or letter). For example, the operator might select Y -> T.

During World War II, German troops used the Enigma to encode strategic messages. During this time, and for several years prior to World War II, many attempted to crack the code. Ultimately, it was the mathematician Alan M. Turing who was able to break the code.

To view the mechanics of the Enigma, visit `https://www.tamdistrict.org/cms/lib/CA01000875/Centricity/Domain/539/Enigma--The%20 Mathematics%20Game.pdf`.

The Enigma provided a solid way to encrypt data. However, when computers entered the picture, and we started using digital data, scientists started to explore ways to protect the confidentiality and integrity of our information. Let's explore this in the next section.

Entering the digital age

Throughout the 1960s and 1970s, computers started populating offices, industry, and government organizations. It soon became apparent that it was necessary to protect data in some way from prying eyes.

However, several decades earlier, the concept of encrypting data was already in the works. In this section, we'll learn how Claude Shannon, an American mathematician and cryptographer, outlined how to encrypt digital data. We'll then examine the beginnings of the DES, with the development of the Feistel and Lucifer ciphers in the 1970s, as scientists recognized the need to secure digital data.

Let's begin by learning about Shannon and his contributions to the field of computing and cryptography.

Innovating in the field of computing

In 1941, Claude Shannon was a young scientist working at Bell Telephone Laboratories (Bell Labs). Shannon worked at Bell Labs conducting research on Boolean algebra and circuit switching. The research would be instrumental in the development of telephone systems during the first half of the 1900s.

> **Important note**
>
> Shannon was an innovator in the field of computing and artificial intelligence. Early on, he provided the insight that digital equipment (computers) should use a binary value, either a 1 or a 0 (true or false), to communicate efficiently. Shannon expanded his research in binary, and coupled that with Boolean logic, which helped him to become a leader in the digital revolution.

Shannon also worked on classified military projects throughout World War II. One of his more influential projects was that on cryptography. In 1941, Shannon wrote *A Mathematical Theory of Cryptography*, which at the time was classified. The paper was later shortened, declassified, and published in 1949. This work solidified cryptography as a science and revolutionized the field.

Shannon stressed the importance of confusion and diffusion when encrypting text. The concepts are the foundation of contemporary block ciphers, and are outlined as follows:

- **Confusion** is obscuring any connection between the unencrypted text, the resultant ciphertext, and the key.

- **Diffusion** distributes the influence of the unencrypted text or key across as much of the resultant ciphertext as feasible.

When encrypting text, confusion and diffusion is achieved using successive rounds of substitution and permutations of the bits (or characters):

- **Substitution** substitutes or switches one bit (or character) for another.

- **Permutation** transforms or rearranges the order of the bits (or characters).

Keep in mind, during a digital transformation, the bits will be transformed; however, when doing a manual transformation, such as the Caesar shift, the characters will be manipulated.

Let's take a look at each of these concepts, starting with substitution.

Substituting values

Substitution can be achieved by using a substitution or S-BOX, also called a lookup table, which replaces characters and satisfies Shannon's property of confusion.

Let's step through an example of how we use the S-BOX to substitute bits (or characters):

1. We start with an input array that holds the initial values, as shown on the left. We also need the S-BOX that provides the values to substitute, as shown on the right in the following diagram:

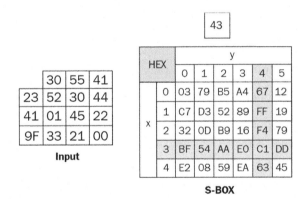

Figure 2.11 – The initial state

2. Next, we see the first value from the input array, 43, is mapped to column 4 row 3 in the S-BOX:

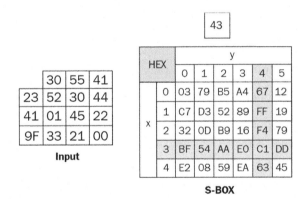

Figure 2.12 – Using the S-BOX to replace the value 43

3. Once the first value is substituted, this then becomes C1 in the input table:

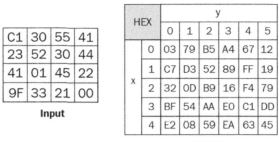

C1	30	55	41
23	52	30	44
41	01	45	22
9F	33	21	00

Input

HEX				y			
		0	1	2	3	4	5
x	0	03	79	B5	A4	67	12
	1	C7	D3	52	89	FF	19
	2	32	0D	B9	16	F4	79
	3	BF	54	AA	E0	C1	DD
	4	E2	08	59	EA	63	45

S-BOX

Figure 2.13 – The input box replaced with the first value, C1

4. The rest of the values for the input box are then replaced, which now completes the substitution.

Next let's take a look at how we can provide permutation.

Grasping permutation

During permutation, the bits (or characters) will transform from their original order. One way to achieve permutation is by using a circular shift.

A circular shift is a basic concept that shifts the bits (or characters) either to the left or to the right.

Let's start with an example of a left circular shift.

Shifting to the left

For a left circular shift for x bits (or characters), where x represents the number of bits (or characters), you would do the following:

- Remove x bits (or characters) from the left and append the bits (or characters) to the right.
- Shift the remaining bits (or characters) to the *left*:

  Input: **00**010111

  Shift to the left 2: 010111**00**

Now let's reverse the process to achieve a right circular shift.

Shifting to the right

For a right circular shift for *x* bits (or characters), where *x* represents the number of bits (or characters), you would do the following:

- Remove *x* bits (or characters) from the right and append the bits (or characters) to the left.

- Shift the remaining bits (or characters) to the *right*:

  Input: 00010011

  Shift to the right 2: **11**000100

To check your work, visit `https://www.browserling.com/tools/rotate-binary`.

Throughout the years, Shannon's influence has provided a template for cryptographic techniques. Next, let's learn how scientists in the 1970s used Shannon's tenets to develop some early ciphers.

Developing the early ciphers

In the 1970s, computers began to infiltrate industry, universities, and government. During that time, much of the data protection and restrictions started with the military, as they were the first to classify data.

Data was labeled according to its sensitivity; for example, data could be considered top secret, secret, or classified. The United States Government started to take a greater interest in protecting data. Scientists David E. Bell and Leonard J. La Padula (Bell-La Padula) published a paper in 1976 on access control, to provide data confidentiality and integrity.

Around the same time, in 1973, at IBM, scientist Horst Feistel developed a block cipher, which was called the Feistel cipher. Feistel outlined a structure that used successive and repeatable rounds on each block, to adhere to Shannon's principles of substitution and permutation.

The Feistel cipher is not a specific cipher; rather, it provides a basis or template for a block cipher design. It provides an elegant and simple encryption technique that is significant in that most modern block ciphers, including the DES, mimic the Feistel structure.

To see a more detailed illustration of the Feistel cipher, you can visit `http://homepages.math.uic.edu/~leon/mcs425-s08/handouts/feistal-diagram.pdf`.

As part of early experiments in cryptographic techniques at IBM, Feistel and his colleagues used the structure to develop the Lucifer cipher. Lucifer used a 128-bit key to encrypt 128 bits block of text and is the precursor of the DES.

We'll learn more about the Feistel and Lucifer ciphers, along with the DES, when we cover symmetric encryption in *Chapter 4, Introducing Symmetric Encryption.*

Summary

In this chapter, we learned about some of the early uses of encryption. We saw how primitive methods such as tattoos, along with tools such as the scytale, were used to conceal information. We then took a closer look at the differences between a monoalphabetic and polyalphabetic cipher and outlined examples of both. We discovered how, throughout the centuries, military leaders sought ways to send and receive messages to their allies during times of war or conflict. Methods to send messages included using dogs, along with homing pigeons, telegraph, telephones, and radio.

Along with the advances in technology came the threat of someone intercepting the messages. As we moved into the digital age, scientist Claude Shannon helped shape the field of computing and cryptography. We learned how substitution and permutation could provide confusion and diffusion during encryption. We then learned how the Feistel cipher provides the template for most modern block ciphers. We saw how the Feistel structure was used to develop the Lucifer cipher, and then DES, as scientists recognized the need to secure digital data.

In the next chapter, we'll compare the different types of attacks that threaten the security of our data. We'll outline the two main types: passive attacks, such as reconnaissance attacks, and active attacks, designed to destroy, steal, modify, or disrupt services or data. So that you can understand why it's necessary to protect data, we'll outline how data exists either in an organization or with an individual, and how not providing sufficient defense methods can lead to an attack and the exposure of sensitive data. Finally, you'll see how it's essential to keep data in its original form. We'll then discover how using encryption can ensure data integrity.

Questions

Now it's time to check your knowledge. Select the best response, then check your answers, found in the *Assessment* section at the end of the book:

1. The ___ used a carefully constructed block of wood and a thin strip of parchment with lettering on the parchment to conceal information.

    a. Enigma

    b. Blaise

    c. scytale

    d. Prussian

2. A monoalphabetic _____ cipher uses a single alphabet and substitutes one letter or character for another. Characters can include letters and special characters, along with punctuation marks.

    a. allocation

    b. substitution

    c. transposition

    d. Blaise

3. An example of a polyalphabetic cipher is the _____ cipher, which uses more than one alphabet to encode text.

    a. Vigenère

    b. Caesar

    c. scytale

    d. Prussian

4. The telephone was invented by Alexander Graham Bell in _____.

    a. 1923

    b. 1861

    c. 1917

    d. 1876

5. Shortly after the end of World War I, a German engineer, Arthur Scherbius, developed the _____, a mechanical device that was capable of creating strong coded messages.

    a. Enigma

    b. Caesar

    c. Blaise

    d. Parker

6. For a right circular shift of 3 bits using the input value of 10011010, the result would be _____.

    a. 00011110

    b. 11011100

    c. 11010100

    d. 01010011

7. The _____ cipher is a precursor the Data Encryption Standard.

    a. Lucifer

    b. Porta

    c. Basta

    d. Blaise

Further reading

Please refer to the following links for more information:

- For a review of some ancient uses of encryption, go to `https://medium.com/tokenring/ancient-uses-of-cryptography-four-examples-that-pre-date-the-internet-14679ae4f509`.

- Take a closer look at ancient languages and their origins by visiting `https://www.ancient-origins.net/artifacts-ancient-writings/hidden-hieroglyphs-ancient-egyptian-lost-language-006653`.

- Read more on the revolt against Darius here: `https://storytellershat.com/2017/11/13/the-tattoo-which-sparked-the-ionian-revolt/`.

- Learn how the Spartans concealed messages using a scytale by visiting `ozscience.com/technology/a-scytale-cryptography-of-the-ancient-sparta/`.

- Read an excerpt from *Jewish Literacy in Roman Palestine*: `https://books.google.com/books?id=zlrxbYml2ioC&pg=PA23&hl=en#v=onepage&q&f=false` to gain insight on the literacy rate during the time period around the 4th century BCE.

- Try out the Porta cipher by going to `http://practicalcryptography.com/ciphers/porta-cipher/`.

- Learn more about the Vigenère cipher, and try the cipher yourself, at `http://practicalcryptography.com/ciphers/classical-era/vigenere-gronsfeld-and-autokey/`.

- Visit the Computer Museum of America to see an image of the Enigma: `https://www.computermuseumofamerica.org/2020/02/25/cmoa-unveils-rare-enigma-machine/`.

- To encrypt data using an Enigma simulator, visit `https://cryptii.com/pipes/enigma-machine`.

3
Evaluating Network Attacks

In today's information superhighway, there is a voluminous amount of data housed on our systems, and traveling over networks and the internet. Because of this, we must face the fact that it's not a matter of *whether* there will be an attack, it's a matter of *when* an attack will occur. The reality is that not all attacks are the same. In this chapter, we'll outline how a network can fall victim to either a passive or active attack, and we'll review examples of both. We'll see that while a passive attack may not seem serious, it can be a precursor to an active attack.

In addition, we'll see that there are many attack vectors that, if not properly protected, can lead to data exfiltration or exposure of confidential information. You'll learn that, today, data is in many places and is growing at an exponential rate, and with this growth comes a greater need to protect the data. Finally, you'll get a better understanding of the meaning of risk, threats, and vulnerabilities. You'll then appreciate how reducing risk in an organization helps prevent data from being changed, destroyed, or lost in an unauthorized or accidental manner.

In this chapter, we're going to cover the following main topics:

- Comparing passive and active attacks
- Protecting sensitive data
- Maintaining integrity

Comparing passive and active attacks

An attack on an information system can be against any of the following services: confidentiality, integrity, availability, or authentication. To further define the types of attacks, there are two broad categories, passive and active:

- **Passive attacks** do not interfere with the system or data integrity, and include activity such as scanning or eavesdropping using packet analysis.

- **Active attacks** seek to disrupt services, modify, steal, or destroy data, and include attacks such as a **Denial of Service** (**DoS**) attack, or releasing malware.

In this section, we'll compare each of the categories and provide some examples of each, along with ways to protect against the various attacks.

Let's start with a discussion on passive attacks.

Carrying out a passive attack

With an active attack, there may be some network instability, system disruption, or data modification. However, with a passive attack, the objective is to do the following:

- Conduct a reconnaissance exercise to monitor and observe the network traffic for information on network devices.

- Capture sensitive information that is in plain text, such as usernames and passwords.

Let's see what's involved during reconnaissance.

Conducting reconnaissance

Before launching an active attack, a malicious actor might conduct a reconnaissance exercise to find out more information on the target network. This is achieved by scanning the network using a variety of tools that help identify weaknesses or vulnerabilities on network hosts.

During reconnaissance, an attacker might scan the network using one of several scans to obtain more information about the network. Let's take a look at some examples of network scans next.

Scanning the network

One of the first types of scans that are done during reconnaissance is called a *ping sweep*.

> **Important note**
>
> The term "ping" is related to the concept of using **sound navigation ranging** (**SONAR**). SONAR can sound like a "ping" when used underwater to identify the presence of objects or life forms.

When using a ping sweep, the malicious actor will use an app to send out a series of **Internet Control Message Protocol** (**ICMP**) packets to see whether any hosts are up and responding. As shown in the following diagram, one of the hosts on the Local Area Network responds:

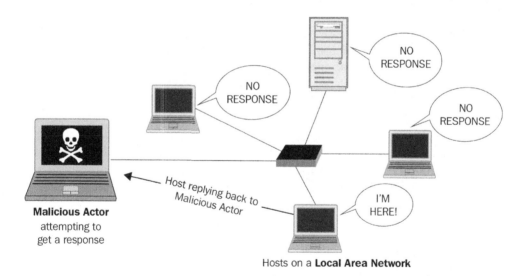

Figure 3.1 – Malicious actor using a ping sweep

Once the attacker identifies a host that is up and responding, the next step is to use a *port scan* to see whether the host has any **Transmission Control Protocol** (**TCP**) ports that are open and listening. The port scan generally scans the well-known ports that are in the range 1-1023; however, the malicious actor can set the app to scan a larger range.

As shown in the following diagram, the port scan will query a responding host, and then report back to the malicious actor on which ports are open:

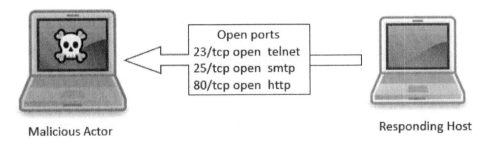

Figure 3.2 – A host responding to a port scan

> **Important note**
> A host with open ports can be a vulnerability. If, while scanning the network, a malicious actor discovers open ports, they might seek to take the next step and connect with the host by using the open port. To mitigate this vulnerability, the network administrator should disable any ports that aren't required.

Another scan that helps to learn more about the network and identify vulnerabilities is **operating system** (**OS**) **fingerprinting**. Fingerprinting gathers information and then makes a best guess as to what OS is in use on each host. As shown in the following diagram, the OS of the responding host is identified as Windows 10:

Figure 3.3 – Identifying a host during OS fingerprinting

Many times, while performing the various scans, the software will also map the network and create a map of the topology. Also called **network mapping**, this scan builds a map that identifies all hosts on the network:

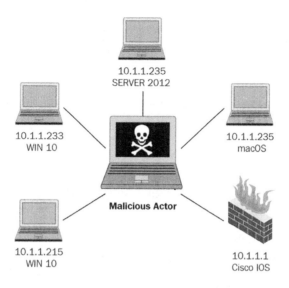

Figure 3.4 – Results from mapping the network

For scanning the network, there are a variety of tools available today. One well-known tool is called **Network Mapper (Nmap)**, which is a free, open source scanner that can identify listening hosts and determine open ports. As shown in the following screenshot, the Nmap scan shows the open and listening ports on host 10.0.0.167:

```
Nmap scan report for 10.0.0.167
Host is up (0.0034s latency).
Not shown: 983 closed ports
PORT      STATE SERVICE
80/tcp    open  http
139/tcp   open  netbios-ssn
443/tcp   open  https
445/tcp   open  microsoft-ds
631/tcp   open  ipp
6839/tcp  open  unknown
7435/tcp  open  unknown
8080/tcp  open  http-proxy
8089/tcp  open  unknown
9102/tcp  open  jetdirect
9110/tcp  open  unknown
9111/tcp  open  DragonIDSConsole
9220/tcp  open  unknown
9290/tcp  open  unknown
MAC Address: 08:2E:5F:F2:32:18 (Hewlett Packard)
```

Figure 3.5 – Nmap scan report for host 10.0.0.167

> **Important note**
> You can find out more information on Nmap at `https://nmap.org/`.
> In addition, you can find out how to close or disable unused ports by doing
> a search on `close or disable unused TCP ports`.

The reconnaissance scans aren't always done in any particular order; however, the ping sweep is generally completed before a port scan. In addition, depending on the objective, there may only be one scan that is run.

> **Important note**
> Many of the same tools used by malicious actors are also used by network
> administrators to monitor the network.

When scanning the network, the app will often generate activity, as many of the scans use protocols, generally TCP and ICMP, to attempt to communicate with other hosts.

However, in some cases, a passive attack does not generate any activity. The attacker might simply eavesdrop on the network by using packet analysis. Packet analysis is also called **sniffing**, and is used to gather network traffic to obtain information that is traveling across the network. Next, let's see how an attacker can use packet sniffing to obtain information.

Sniffing network traffic

Packet sniffing can be done using software such as **Wireshark**, an open source packet analysis tool. During this exercise, the attacker can obtain a variety of information that can include network device configuration, or even sensitive information.

Sniffing network traffic can help the attacker learn the types and versions of devices on the network. This is possible because some devices communicate with one another and offer information about their OS, hostname, **Internet Protocol** (**IP**) address, and other information specific to that device. Protocols such as **Cisco Discovery Protocol** (**CDP**) and **Simple Service Discovery Protocol** (**SSDP**) provide information that can help the attacker learn about network devices.

Eavesdropping using packet sniffing is done in order to try and capture interesting data, such as a phone call, credentials, email, or documents. By using Wireshark to monitor the traffic, they might be able to obtain a username and password that is sent across the network.

For example, in the following screenshot, we see within the stream a username (`admin@google.com`) and a password (`Password2010`), being sent in plain text:

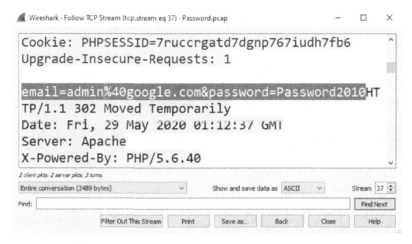

Figure 3.6 – Username and password

> **Important note**
>
> When you see %40 in the email address, this translates to the @ symbol. For more details, visit `https://grox.net/utils/encoding.html`.

To defend against packet sniffing, data should be encrypted. However, not all devices encrypt traffic when communicating on the network, which can lead to exposure of information.

During a passive attack, the victim may not be aware that anything is happening. However, a passive attack can be dangerous as it can identify system weaknesses and be a precursor to an active attack.

Next, let's see an overview on the types of active attacks that can take place.

Launching an active attack

An active attack seeks to destroy, steal, or modify the integrity of a system. The types of attacks can vary, and each type can have a different objective. In an active attack, system resources and/or data can be damaged or destroyed, which can affect normal operations. Common attacks include *social engineering*, *malware*, and *DoS* attacks.

Social engineering is commonly used by cybercriminals to get a victim to perform some action. They may try to encourage them to click on a link to visit a web page, or prompt them to sign into a bank site to check account information. This takes advantage of an individual's trusting nature, and includes techniques such as phishing, pharming, popups, and fake websites. Social engineering is dangerous, and is the leading cause of ransomware attacks.

Another attack commonly used is malware, which continues to improve in sophistication in order to get into our systems. Let's outline the different types of malware next.

Understanding malware

Malware is malicious software and includes the following:

- **Rootkits** provide a backdoor into a system to allow access to a host.

- **Spyware** records activities such as keystrokes, screenshots, authentication credentials, and other information, and sends the data to a remote site.

- **Trojans** appear as useful programs or utilities; however, concealed within the program or utility, there is code that allows the cybercriminal to take control of the victim's computer remotely.

- **Viruses** can self-replicate yet need a way to propagate to other hosts. *Worms* are a virus subclass that can spread on their own. Both can cause a range of activity, such as consuming system resources that can slow or even halt tasks.

- **Ransomware** prevents access to a system, generally by using some form of encryption, and holds the system hostage until some type of ransom is paid.

Every day, hundreds of thousands of new malware variants are discovered, as seen in this chart: `https://www.av-test.org/en/statistics/malware/`. In addition, much of the malware today is polymorphic, in that it changes its form and behavior to elude detection. This makes it even harder to protect against ongoing threats.

Another threat is a DoS attack, which prevents legitimate requests from accessing the server. Let's take a look.

Locking out legitimate users

A DoS attack sends hundreds of requests per second to a target system. More commonly known as a **Distributed Denial of Service (DDoS)**, this attack uses hundreds of thousands of bots (or zombies). The goal is to flood the system with so many bogus requests that legitimate users are locked out.

To launch a DoS attack, a cybercriminal first needs an army of bots. The malicious actor creates the army by first infecting millions of unknowing hosts with malware so they become zombies, which then become part of a large botnet. The botnet is controlled by a **Command and Control (C&C)** server. The attack occurs when, at a predefined time, or at a go signal from the C&C server, the zombies launch an attack on an unsuspecting victim.

The reality is that attacks can occur at any layer of the **Open System Interconnection (OSI)** model. Today, there are many different types of cyber threats; some are lesser known, and some are older. However, malicious actors will try all exploits to gain control of a system, as they may feel our defenses are down, or we may have forgotten about the exploit.

The key is, anything is possible, and over the years, we have seen an escalation of cyberattacks, which has resulted in businesses losing billions of dollars.

As a result, it's imperative for businesses to understand all possible attack vectors. Once the attack vectors are identified, the next step is to lock down and defend the organization. Doing so will reduce the effect of an attack and subsequent exposure of sensitive data. Let's explore this concept next.

Protecting sensitive data

Because of the expanding networks, additional devices, and the **Internet of Things (IoT)**, data is in many places. Data lives within an organization, on storage devices, or even in our cars and homes, and is growing at an exponential rate. Along with this growth comes the real concern of the threat of unauthorized access to data.

Many individuals feel that data is the *new gold*. Cybercriminals are constantly seeking ways to gain access to our data, for a variety of reasons. Reasons include data theft, along with a newer threat, data modification. Unlike theft, data modification seeks to alter the integrity of data, for example, changing the details of blueprints or intellectual property.

In this section, we'll take a look at the many attack vectors that provide a way for data to be compromised in some way. Then we'll take a look at a few key methods to defend against data loss or modification.

Let's start with a discussion of the ways someone can gain access to data.

Understanding attack vectors

An **attack vector** is a path or means by which a malicious actor can access a system. Today, there are many attack vectors, including storage devices, email, mobile devices, cloud storage, malware, wireless networks, and the user.

Data exists in a variety of locations, within an organization, in the cloud, on storage devices, and computer systems. When not at rest on a storage medium, it is in motion over the network, or held in memory. Wherever it exists, there is a threat that someone can gain access and modify or extract the data in some way.

When dealing with data, there are a few main concerns. We need to ensure data is kept in the following way:

- **Confidential**,which protects against unauthorized disclosure
- **Unaltered**, which ensures that data is not modified, lost, or destroyed
- **Available**, which ensures data can be accessed by authorized objects

It's important to be aware of the many ways someone or something can gain access to data, so you can take steps to employ appropriate security mechanisms.

Some of the attack vectors include the following:

- **Mobile devices**: Our small, handheld devices contain our photos, contacts, and apps that allow us to shop, bank, and communicate. Malicious actors target vulnerable mobile devices as a way to a more lucrative target, such as a corporate intranet.
- **Wireless networks**: These provide an attractive attack vector as Wi-Fi is characteristically insecure. Malicious actors tempt users to join open access points located in coffee shops and airports, to gain information such as usernames and passwords.
- **The user**: This is the most vulnerable attack vector as it is the weakest link in any system. Every day, millions of people around the world fall victim to some sort of cybercrime, including scams, malware, phishing attacks, and credit card fraud.

A malicious actor will go through a process to gain control of a system, as shown in the following diagram:

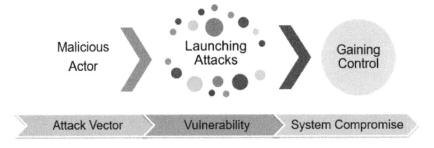

Figure 3.7 – The process of moving from an attack vector to system compromise

The steps to gain access to a system are as follows:

1. The process begins by a malicious actor seeking out a vulnerable target, by using one of many attack vectors.

2. Once identified, the malicious actor will exploit the vulnerability, by launching an attack (or multiple attacks), to gain access to the system.

3. After the malicious actor gains control of the system, the next step is to extract sensitive information, including passwords or credit card data.

4. The malicious actor might even create a backdoor on the compromised system so they can return to access the system at a later date.

We now see the many attack vectors that can allow a malicious actor to gain access to a system. The next step is to outline the ways we can prevent data loss.

Providing defense mechanisms

While no defense method is totally threatproof, good practices will help hamper a potential attack. Most experts generally suggest using a layered approach with a variety of proven methods.

Defense mechanisms include logical and physical security and security appliances, along with policies that outline proper behavior. The mechanisms are defined as follows:

*   **Logical security** includes access control techniques that ensure **authentication, authorization, and accounting** (**AAA**) in an information system.

*   **Physical security** methods limit access to buildings and equipment by using physical controls such as locks, lighting, gates, and smartcards.

*   **Security appliances** include intrusion detection/prevention systems, gateways, and firewalls that are tuned to allow or deny traffic based on a set of rules.

*   **Policies** define a set of rules of conduct for anyone or anything that interacts with the system resources. Policies can include topics such as password complexity, antivirus guidelines, or user education.

Logical network defenses, security appliances, and anti-malware protection continue to improve in their ability to defend systems. Many devices have built-in **artificial intelligence** (**AI**) that monitors the network and quickly identifies unusual or suspicious behavior, and then sends an alert. This then helps the network administrator to be more responsive.

Let's take a look at how a layered defense combines protection methods to help prevent attacks.

Using a layered approach

When we layer our defenses, we use more than one method to defend against attacks. For example, imagine an attacker trying to get malware onto a server. They may be able to do the following:

1. Provide stolen credentials and get authenticated on the network.
2. Pass through the firewall and head to the server.

However, once at the server, they would be stopped by the anti-malware protection, as shown in the following diagram:

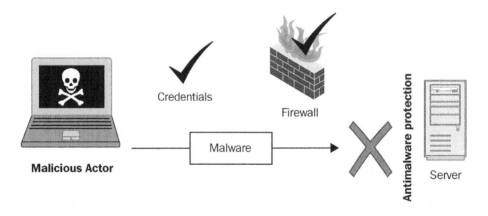

Figure 3.8 – Using a layered approach to provide enhanced security

As we can see, malicious activity might be able to spoof a system or circumvent a firewall. That is why a layered defense posture helps provide protection in case one or more defense methods fail.

In addition to the protection methods already in place, an organization should create security policies. Policies help maintain a structure for the management and administration of the security of the network.

Let's see what's involved when creating security policies.

Creating and maintaining policies

Policies are designed to protect the infrastructure, by defining how an organization's people, processes, and devices access and interact with system resources. When creating policies, the organization should create a security plan, then policies and procedures, as shown in the following diagram:

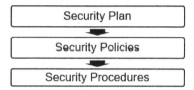

Figure 3.9 – Progression from plan to procedures

For an optimal security posture, the progression should go as follows:

1. The key stakeholders should sit down and think about the overall security posture of an organization, and then create a *security plan*. To see a set of guidelines that can help with this process, visit `https://nvlpubs.nist.gov/nistpubs/Legacy/SP/nistspecialpublication800-18r1.pdf`.

2. From the findings determined when creating the security plan, the team will develop *security policies* that define rules of proper behavior using an interdepartmental team approach.

3. If required, the team should develop *security procedures* that define the way the policy should be executed.

Keep the policies in line with the objectives of the organization. In addition, it's best to have the support of upper-level management during their creation. You'll want to consider the following when creating the policies:

-   **Who is the audience?** Is the policy designed for trade workers, middle management, or consultants who work with the system?

-   **How should the policy be shared?** Will you share the policy by sending an email or use a paper memo that is displayed in a common area?

-   **What is the key message?** What is the policy is trying to convey, for example, use of passwords, internet access, or acceptable use?

-   **Is the policy driven by regulations?** If so, management should outline a clear definition of the requirements involved and the rationale.

The team should write the policy using clear and concise language with no use of jargon. Once written and approved, you'll need to disseminate the policy and train all users. In addition, it's best to assign responsibility to monitor, enforce, and periodically review the policy.

Creating a security policy can be overwhelming, but there is help. `SANS.org` is a respected source for information security training. They have some templates that are free to use and will step you through the process. To see an extensive list, visit `https://www.sans.org/information-security-policy`.

As outlined, policies help define proper behavior. However, writing and implementing policies isn't always enough. It's also important to train your users, so they can act as a human firewall. Let's take a look.

Strengthening the human firewall

As logical and physical system defenses improve, malicious actors use social engineering to try and penetrate a softer target: the people in an organization, including employees, customers, and contractors. A skilled malicious actor will most likely use social engineering to obtain access to a system, before using more complex methods, such as password cracking.

To protect against a social engineering attack, put in place a solid user education program for new and existing employees. Discuss good practice guidelines when dealing with system resources, including the following:

- Don't click on suspicious links in an email or online.
- Use caution when using public Wi-Fi networks.
- Secure your mobile devices.
- Change your password often and don't use the same password for all sites.

Run periodic tests to see whether your employees can be spoofed. Many resources are available online. One site is here at *SonicWall's phishing IQ test*: `https://www.sonicwall.com/en-us/phishing-iq-test-landing`.

Social engineering is one of the hardest threats to defend against as humans can be our weakest link. However, steps can be taken to strengthen the human firewall to better protect the data.

As outlined, the one constant security goal in an organization is to maintain the integrity of the system, by taking steps to prevent a breach. In the next section, let's see how using encryption helps protect the data and decrease the risk of data exposure.

Maintaining integrity

It's essential to keep data in its original, unaltered form. Although there may be threats to the organization, encryption can ensure data integrity and prevent data from being changed, destroyed, or lost in an unauthorized or accidental manner. Organizations seek to protect the data and system resources, by implementing security strategies.

In this section, we'll take a look at just what's at stake, by first outlining the meaning of assets. We'll then clarify the definition of risk, which is a product of threats and vulnerabilities. You'll then understand how decreasing vulnerabilities will reduce overall risk.

Let's start with defining assets.

Protecting assets

When implementing security strategies, an organization seeks to protect their assets from threats such as cyberattacks or theft. Assets are either tangible or intangible goods that can be assigned a value:

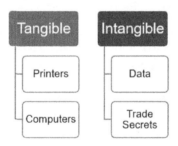

Figure 3.10 – Tangible and intangible assets

Tangible assets are more common and easier to understand as they represent something you can touch. Tangible assets include the following:

- Furniture, cash, and jewelry
- Computers, servers, and printers

Intangible assets are goods that you can't touch or see; however, they still represent value to the company. Intangible assets are more difficult to monetize, but in some ways, they may be more valuable than the tangible assets. Intangible assets include the following:

- Trade secrets, databases, and client lists
- Company records and brand reputation

It's good practice to periodically conduct an inventory of your assets, so you truly understand the value of what you are trying to protect. In the next section, let's define risk, and learn one key strategy for decreasing overall risk.

Managing risk

Risk is the potential that something unpleasant or dangerous can happen. The outcome can range in severity as follows:

- Risk can have a minor (non-catastrophic) outcome. For example, there is a risk you will get wet if you go out in the rain without an umbrella.

- Risk can have a serious outcome, such as a financial loss, disruption to the supply chain, or even loss of life.

Risk is a function of threats and vulnerabilities, according to this formula:

$$\text{Risk} = \text{Threat} \times \text{Vulnerability}$$

Figure 3.11 – Formula to determine risk

A *threat* is an event, object, or individual that is capable of causing harm or damage. Threats can include malware, mischief, human error, and natural disasters. Threats exist; however, they are impossible to control.

A *vulnerability* is a flaw or weakness. When dealing with an information system, a vulnerability can include software bugs, unpatched systems, missing antivirus, or even human behavior. In many cases, we can fix vulnerabilities.

So that you can better understand the three terms in context, we'll use an example of a risk analysis exercise.

Performing a risk assessment

Risk is a function of threats and vulnerabilities. In general, although threats exist, we cannot control them. We can, however, minimize or control the vulnerabilities. Therefore, if we reduce the vulnerabilities, we will reduce overall risk.

To show you how threats and vulnerabilities work together to produce risk, we'll use an example. We'll see how using different levels of antimalware protection on a system will alter the risk:

- One system will be protected using a *free antivirus* with no automatic updates.

- One system will be protected using a *paid antivirus* with automatic updates.

- One system will be protected using a **unified threat management (UTM)** appliance with automatic updates.

In each case, there is a 100% chance that malware will be a threat. Knowing this, let's build our matrix. As shown in the following screenshot, I have assigned each of the systems a vulnerability rating as to how easily malware will infect the system:

Scenario	Risk	=	Threat	X	Vulnerability
Free antivirus	90%	=	100%	X	90%
Paid antivirus	40%	=	100%	X	40%
UTM	10%	=	100%	X	10%

Figure 3.12 – Anti-malware protection – Risk analysis

As illustrated, the system using the free antivirus was the most vulnerable, and the risk of infection was 90%. The system using free antivirus had a 40% risk of being infected. However, the system using the UTM was minimally vulnerable, and therefore had only a 10% risk rating.

When providing security strategies, the goal is to decrease risk. As illustrated, when you decrease the vulnerabilities, you decrease overall risk.

Summary

In this chapter, we examined the differences between active and passive attacks. We saw how a passive attack is done to either learn information about devices on the network, or pick up confidential information, such as usernames and passwords. We then learned the different types of active attacks, which can modify the integrity of our systems and lead to data loss or compromise.

So that you can understand why encryption is so important, we outlined just what is at risk. We learned the different types of attack vectors, and the different defense mechanisms such as logical and physical security, security appliances, along with policies. Finally, we learned how organizations seek to protect assets and maintain system integrity, and how using countermeasures can reduce vulnerabilities and reduce overall risk.

In the next chapter, we'll discover symmetric encryption. We'll start with briefly covering some of the early ciphers, Lucifer and Feistel, and their influence on the **Data Encryption Standard (DES)**. We'll then examine common algorithms including AES, DES, Blowfish, and Twofish. You'll learn the difference between a block and a stream cipher. We'll also cover how a stream cipher has different modes of operation such as **cipher block chaining (CBC)** and **electronic code book (ECB)**. Finally, we'll take a look at how a stream cipher secures wireless communications and discuss some common protocols in use today.

Questions

Now it's time to check your knowledge. Select the best response, then check your answers, found in the *Assessment* section at the end of the book:

1. _____ attacks do not interfere with the system or data integrity and include activity such as scanning or eavesdropping using packet analysis.

    a. Vector

    b. Modified

    c. Active

    d. Passive

2. _____ attacks seek to disrupt services, modify, steal, or destroy data, and include attacks such as **Denial of Service (DoS)** attacks or releasing malware.

    a. Vector

    b. Modified

    c. Active

    d. Passive

3. An attack _____ is a path or means by which a malicious actor can access a system and includes storage devices, email, mobile devices, cloud storage, and malware.

    a. vector

    b. stage

    c. appliance

    d. wall

4. Network _____ that protect our networks include intrusion detection/intrusion prevention systems, along with firewalls that are tuned to allow or deny traffic based on a set of rules.

   a. stages

   b. policies

   c. attacks

   d. appliances

5. A _____ is a flaw or weakness when dealing with an information system, and can include software bugs, unpatched systems, missing antivirus, or even human error.

   a. threat

   b. appliance

   c. vulnerability

   d. cage

6. When you decrease the _____, you decrease overall risk.

   a. threats

   b. vulnerabilities

   c. procedures

   d. attacks

7. _____ is one of the hardest threats to defend against, as humans can be our weakest link.

   a. Social engineering

   b. Cages

   c. Viruses

   d. Worms

Further reading

Please refer to the following links for more information:

- To see a live cyberthreat map, visit `https://threatmap.checkpoint.com/`.

- A good article from Malwarebytes on the Future of Undetected Malware can be found here: `https://resources.malwarebytes.com/files/2018/12/Malwarebytes-Labs-Under-The-Radar-APAC-1.pdf`.

- To see a visual on how quickly the WannaCry ransomware infected tens of thousands of computers, visit `https://nyti.ms/2r9WIfE`.

- An article from Cisco on common cyber attacks: `https://www.cisco.com/c/en/us/products/security/common-cyberattacks.html`.

- For a glossary of threats, visit `https://www.cyren.com/resources/cyber-threat-glossary`.

- An article that outlines a new threat, data manipulation: `https://www.cloudmask.com/blog/is-data-manipulation-the-next-step-in-cybercrime`.

- To see an overview on intangible goods, go to `https://simplicable.com/new/intangible-goods`.

Section 2: Understanding Cryptographic Techniques

In this section, we'll first discuss symmetric encryption along with algorithms such as the **Data Encryption Standard** (**DES**) and **Advanced Encryption Standard** (**AES**). We'll then see how asymmetric encryption uses two keys, and includes algorithms such as **Rivest, Shamir, Adleman** (**RSA**) and **Elliptic Curve Cryptography** (**ECC**). We'll also learn how asymmetric (or public key) encryption can be used in several ways, to secure email, exchange keys, and create a digital signature. Finally, we'll learn how a hash algorithm is a one-way function that outputs a message digest to provide message authentication.

This section comprises the following chapters:

- *Chapter 4, Introducing Symmetric Encryption*
- *Chapter 5, Dissecting Asymmetric Encryption*
- *Chapter 6, Examining Hash Algorithms*

4

Introducing Symmetric Encryption

Today, we use cryptographic algorithms, techniques, and processes to secure our data that is either in motion or at rest. One of the driving factors in this effort is the need for businesses to adhere to standards, such as the **Payment Card Industry Data Security Standard (PCI DSS)**. However, on a personal level, each of us wants to keep our private data just that: private. Every day, malicious actors launch a variety of attacks to try to gain access to our data. Nevertheless, with strong algorithms that are properly implemented, cryptographic tools and techniques will continue to secure our data and transactions.

In this chapter, you'll gain a better understanding of how symmetric encryption quickly and efficiently secures data. We'll see its humble beginnings, with scientist Horst Feistel of **International Business Machines (IBM)** creating the Feistel network, a foundational element for every modern-day block cipher. We'll then discuss some symmetric encryption algorithms, such as the **Data Encryption Standard (DES)** and **Advanced Encryption Standard (AES)**.

We'll compare the differences between a block and a stream cipher. We'll see how a block cipher is able to encrypt any amount of data with minimal overhead. We'll then illustrate that if we add memory to a block cipher, this results in a stream cipher. You'll be able to understand that when using a stream cipher there are several modes of operation, some of which are more secure than others. Finally, we'll see how stream ciphers secure our wireless communications, and discuss protocols, such as **Wi-Fi Protected Access (WPA)**, that are in use today.

In this chapter, we're going to cover the following main topics:

- Discovering the evolution of symmetric encryption
- Outlining symmetric algorithms
- Dissecting block and stream ciphers
- Comparing symmetric encryption operation modes
- Securing wireless communications

Discovering the evolution of symmetric encryption

Today, encryption plays a key role in securing digital data during transactions. This includes everything from online shopping to phone calls, and even messages coming from our watches and other devices that constantly send and receive data. Encryption also protects data at rest, such as data stored in the cloud or on a drive.

Prior to the 1970s, there wasn't much thought about securing digital data. Any data processing was secure in early **Local Area Networks (LANs)**, and the internet was just starting to take shape. However, large organizations began to evaluate the need to secure our data. One such company was IBM, an industry leader in technology. IBM put together a group of scientists to design a solution to protect customer data.

In this section, we'll take a look at some of the motivators behind creating an encryption algorithm to secure data. We'll also discuss the **Feistel cipher**, which is significant as it is essentially the foundation for all modern block ciphers. We'll then see how the Feistel cipher led to the development of Lucifer, which later became DES.

Let's start with a discussion on IBM's early influence on cryptography.

Protecting customer data

IBM's role as a leader in technology began in the late 1880s, with the development of tabulation equipment used for the **United States (US)** census. From those early beginnings, they continued with designing equipment for use in the business and scientific communities.

In the 1960s, IBM created one of the first mainframes, the System/360, which dominated the market for large-scale computing systems. During that time, the chairman of IBM, Thomas J. Watson Jr., assembled a group of scientists to work on cryptography research. The team was led by scientist Horst Feistel, who was a recognized cryptographer.

Concurrently, IBM had a banking application for Lloyds Bank in the **United Kingdom (UK)**. It was then that they began to see the importance of securing customer data. The team went to work on designing a secure algorithm and the result was what is known as the Feistel cipher.

The Feistel cipher is significant and acted as a guide or template for several algorithms. Let's discuss this, next.

Developing the Feistel cipher

Scientists at IBM have been influential in many significant technology-related contributions over the years. The Feistel cipher is one of those noteworthy contributions. As a cryptographic technique, it provides the foundation for other early block ciphers, such as DES. Also referred to as the Feistel network, the cipher is elegant and simple and obeys conventional encryption principles, as outlined by Claude Shannon.

If you recall our discussion on Shannon in *Chapter 3*, *Evaluating Network Attacks*, under the *Innovating the field of computing* section, he stressed the importance of confusion and diffusion when encrypting text. This can be achieved by using successive rounds of substitution and permutation of characters, which are the foundational elements of contemporary block ciphers.

A Feistel network follows a pattern of multiple rounds of processing of the plaintext, each round consisting of substitution followed by permutation. The cipher takes an input of either a 64-bit or a 128-bit block of text and will go through 16 rounds to encrypt the data. The same cipher is run in reverse to decrypt the text.

> **Important note**
>
> When encrypting text using a block cipher, the algorithm might need to include padding to make an even block size. The type of padding will be dependent on the algorithm and can be in the form of random characters, spaces, or zeros.

In the following diagram, we see a single round of the Feistel cipher:

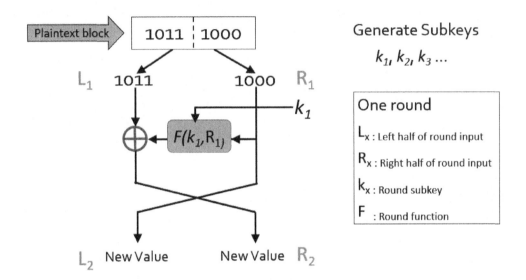

Figure 4.1 – One round of the Feistel cipher

So that you can understand each step of the cipher, we'll step through this example, using a block size of 8 bits and a key size of 6 bits, and encrypt using four rounds. To begin with, we see the following parameters:

- 8-bit block of plaintext: 10111000

- 6-bit key (**K**): 100101

- Number of rounds (**R**): 4

One of the main elements of the cipher is the round function (**F**), as discussed next.

Performing the round function

The round function $F\ (kx,\ Rx)$ involves two simple operations, an **Exclusive OR** (**XOR**) and a left circular shift. Let's see what each of these involves, starting with an XOR.

Using an XOR

If we assume true = 1 and false = 0, the logic for an *XOR* is this:

- **Y** will be true (1) when the inputs **A** or **B** are different from one another (one is true and one is false).

- **Y** will be false (0), when **A** or **B** are the same (both are true or both are false).

The output is shown in the following truth table:

A	B	Y
0	0	0
0	1	1
1	0	1
1	1	0

Figure 4.2 – Truth table for an XOR

For example, an XOR of two values 1011 and 1001 will yield 0010.

Next, let's see how a left circular shift works.

Employing a left circular shift

Shifting of bits or bytes is another common operation. A 1-bit left circular shift moves the bits over so that the leftmost bit *circles* around to the end—for example, the input 0010 will become 0100.

Therefore, performing the round function takes the input of the right side of the block and the corresponding key (kx) and performs an XOR, and then executes a 1-bit left circular shift on the result.

Both the XOR and left circular shift operations are quite simple and, with small enough numbers, can be done using only pencil and paper. This helps provide the simplicity and elegance of a symmetric encryption algorithm.

> **Important note**
>
> In an encryption algorithm, a *round function* can be any computation that ensures adequate confusion and diffusion.

Before encrypting the text, we'll need to create subkeys, as outlined next.

Generating subkeys

Subkeys are shorter keys used to encrypt each round and are derived from the original key K. Because in our example there are four rounds, we'll need four subkeys.

For example, we can identify the 6 bits of the key as b1, b2, b3, b4, b5, and b6.

From our key (K) 10010, we can then generate subkeys (k) using this formula:

- k1 = b1 b2 b3 b4
- k2 = b3 b4 b5 b6
- k3 = b2 b3 b4 b5
- k4 = b1 b2 b5 b6

The resultant subkeys will be as follows:

- k1 = 1001, which will be used in round 1
- k2 = 0101, which will be used in round 2
- k3 = 0010, which will be used in round 3
- k4 = 1001, which will be used in round 4

After generating the subkeys for each round, we are ready to encrypt the text.

Encrypting the text

In this simple example, the process of moving through a single round of encrypting text will progress as follows:

1. The cipher takes a block of text as the input, which is divided into two halves.
2. For each round, the right half of the block remains the same.
3. The left-hand side of the block is transformed using the round function with the data from the right half of the block, and the appropriate subkey.
4. At the completion of the round, each side is swapped.
5. The last round is not swapped.

As you can see, the Feistel cipher is an elegant cipher that efficiently provides substitution and permutation of characters to quickly encrypt the data.

No matter which algorithm you are using, when encrypting data it's important to recognize the following concepts:

- The larger the block size, the greater the security.
- The longer the key length, the greater the security.
- The more rounds, the greater the security.

The Feistel cipher remains significant in its role and influence in the structure of block ciphers. It evolved to become Lucifer, as we'll learn, next.

Creating the Lucifer cipher

The IBM team developed the Lucifer cipher to protect data within a cash dispensing system used by Lloyds Bank. The system was an early version of what is known as an **automatic teller machine (ATM)**, in use today. You can read more on this here:

`https://www.ibm.com/ibm/history/ibm100/us/en/icons/bankauto/`

IBM was not the only entity concerned about creating ways to protect data. In the late 1960s, the US **National Bureau of Standards (NBS)** began evaluating the need to protect consumer and government data. This research evolved into a recognized need to create a national standard to secure data.

> **Important note**
> The NBS became the **National Institute of Standards and Technology (NIST)** in 1988.

In 1973, the NBS presented a formal request to the public for an encryption algorithm. The specifications stated that the algorithm must have the following characteristics:

- A high level of security
- An efficient and elegant design
- The ability to be understood
- An adaptable nature
- Be economical and exportable

At this point, the scientists at IBM felt the perfect candidate was a refined version of Lucifer. IBM submitted the algorithm, and it was accepted. However, after evaluating Lucifer, the **National Security Agency (NSA)** made some modifications, detailed as follows:

- The key length was reduced from 128 bits to 56 bits.
- The inner workings were slightly modified.

This then became DES, which was adopted in 1977 as the government standard for encrypting data.

> **Important note**
> The **Data Encryption Standard (DES)** is also known as the **Data Encryption Algorithm (DEA)**.

After releasing DES, this prompted a lot of research in cryptography. At this point, the only encryption algorithms were in the form of symmetric algorithms, until the development of asymmetric or public-key encryption in 1976.

Let's explore symmetric algorithms, next.

Outlining symmetric algorithms

When designing a cryptographic algorithm, the idea is to have an elegant and efficient cipher that secures data with an appropriate amount of confusion and diffusion. In this segment, we'll review the elements that make symmetric encryption computationally fast and capable of efficiently performing the calculations necessary to encrypt data. We'll then review AES, DES, and other algorithms used in a production network. We'll finish with a discussion on how the keys to be used in each round or iteration during encryption are generated.

Let's start by discussing the key concepts in symmetric encryption.

Understanding symmetric encryption

The term *symmetric* means balanced or equal, which is a fitting description for symmetric encryption as it uses the same shared secret key to encrypt and decrypt text.

Symmetric encryption, also called conventional or secret key encryption, is done in a straightforward manner, using the following five main components:

- **Plaintext** is data that can be read or understood, as there is nothing to conceal the true nature of the data.

- A **shared secret key** is a key that both parties must share, as the key is used to encrypt and decrypt the text.

- An **encryption algorithm** is what is used to provide substitution and permutation of the text.

- **Ciphertext** is data that cannot be read or understood unless you have a key to decrypt the data.

- A **decryption algorithm** is the encryption algorithm run in reverse.

The process of encrypting text using symmetric encryption is shown in the following diagram:

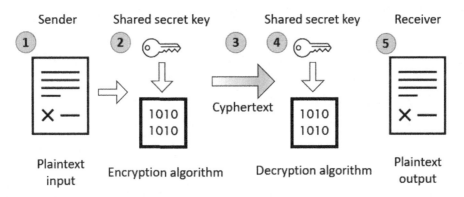

Figure 4.3 – Symmetric encryption process

Let's step through the process of encrypting data, as follows:

1. We begin with the plaintext (data) input on the sender's side.

2. The plaintext is encrypted using the shared secret key and the encryption algorithm.

3. The ciphertext is sent to the recipient.

4. The ciphertext is decrypted using the shared secret key and the decryption algorithm.

5. The resultant plaintext (or data) is presented to the receiver.

While there are several symmetric algorithms, the first US standard was DES. Let's explore this, next.

Describing the Data Encryption Standard

DES is a minor variation of the Lucifer cipher, which became the first US government standard for encrypting data in 1977. DES encrypts a 64-bit block of data using a 56-bit key. From the 56-bit key, 16 subkeys are generated, and a corresponding 16 rounds of processing are used to encrypt the data.

The key in DES is 56 bits. However, in some documentation, you may see the key being referenced as 64 bits. The reality is that every eighth bit is a parity bit that is not used as part of the key. However, this parity bit may be used to detect errors. As shown in the following screenshot, every eighth bit is omitted:

1	2	3	4	5	6	7	8	9	10	11	12	13	14	15	16
17	18	19	20	21	22	23	24	25	26	27	28	29	30	31	32
33	34	35	36	37	38	39	40	41	42	43	44	45	46	47	48
49	50	51	52	53	54	55	56	57	58	59	60	61	62	63	64

Figure 4.4 – The DES key with every eighth bit omitted

What results is a 56-bit key and 8 parity bits, and that is how you get 64 bits.

Next, let's outline how DES encrypts data.

Encrypting with DES

The encryption process starts with a block of 64-bit text as the input and will go through 16 rounds, as shown in the following diagram:

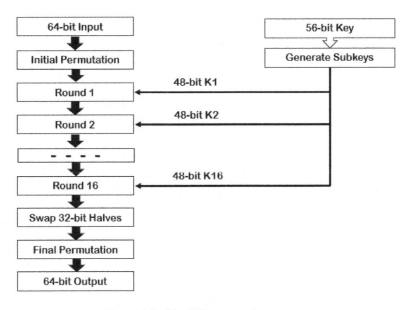

Figure 4.5 – The DES encryption process

On the left-hand side of the preceding diagram, the process is as follows:

1. The algorithm takes a 64-bit block of data and performs an initial permutation, whereby the algorithm rearranges the bits and then splits the block into two 32-bit halves.

2. The process goes through 16 rounds. At the end of the 16 rounds, the two 32-bit halves are rejoined.

3. The data then moves through a final permutation and becomes a 64-bit block of data as the output.

On the right-hand side of the diagram, we see where the algorithm takes the 56-bit key and generates 16 subkeys, one for each round.

Although many felt DES was effective in encrypting text, scientists soon began to scrutinize the algorithm's security, as we'll learn next.

Voicing security concerns

DES had been used to encrypt and secure data since its standardization. However, along with the widespread use of DES, many began to voice a few key concerns, outlined here:

- The 56-bit key size was a potential target for a brute-force attack.

- The parity bit was questioned as well, as it provided no measurable improvement in the encryption process.

As a result, in the late 1990s, scientists felt a way to overcome this concern was to use three iterations of DES. The result was called **Triple DES** (**3DES**), which increased the key length to 168 bits and preserved the use of DES. However, because of the way 3DES encrypts data, the algorithm is slow and clumsy.

Both DES and 3DES are still in use by some applications; however, they are considered insecure and should be avoided if possible.

A better alternative is the AES, which we'll learn about next.

Illustrating the Advanced Encryption Standard

DES had been used worldwide to secure digital data since 1977. While the threat of someone being able to brute-force the short key was mitigated with the development of 3DES, NIST felt it was time to issue a new standard. The goal of the new algorithm was that it would be able to take us into the next generation of processing and be able to withstand a brute-force attack.

In the fall of 1997, NIST issued a request for candidate algorithms to be selected as the new standard. The requirements were similar to those specified when selecting candidates in the 1970s. The requirements included that the algorithm be a flexible, efficient, and economical symmetric block cipher. However, because of lessons learned with DES, new requirements outlined that the algorithm must be able to meet the following criteria:

- Support a block size of 128 bits

- Have key lengths of 128, 192, and 256 bits

From a dozen participants, NIST selected the Rijndael algorithm, which was renamed the AES. In 2002, AES then became the new US standard for encrypting data.

Let's learn how AES encrypts data, next.

Breaking down AES

Unlike the Feistel cipher and DES, whereby the data is encrypted by working through a round and then swapping sides, Rijndael moves a 128-bit block of text through four main transformations.

Several transformations are performed using bytes. AES performs the following, which provides substitution and permutation of the data:

- **Substitute bytes**: This provides substitution.
- **Shift rows**: This provides permutation.
- **Mix columns**: This provides permutation.
- **Add round key**: This performs an XOR operation.

The data moves through each of the four transformations, which represents one round. All transformations are completed except during the last round, where the mix-columns process is not done.

AES begins with a 128-bit block of plaintext, which is equal to 16 bytes, which is calculated in the following manner:

- One (1) byte is equal to eight (8) bits.
- 128 bits divided by eight (8) is equal to 16 bytes.

The algorithm then segments each byte (denoted by **b** here), and then populates the state table in a block formation, as follows:

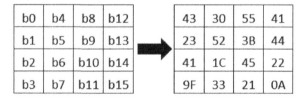

Figure 4.6 – Populating the AES state table

Important note

Each byte in the state table is represented as two hexadecimal characters. This works in the following manner:

One (1) byte is equal to eight (8) bits.

One hexadecimal character is equal to four (4) bits

Two hexadecimal characters are equal to one byte.

AES encrypts the text using a set of four operations that varies from 9 to 11 rounds. The number of rounds will depend on the key length, as follows:

- The 128-bit key will complete 10 rounds.
- The 192-bit key will complete 12 rounds.
- The 256-bit key will complete 14 rounds.

Similar to DES, the subkeys are created from the original key, and then the corresponding subkeys are used during each round.

Encrypting data using AES is represented in the following manner:

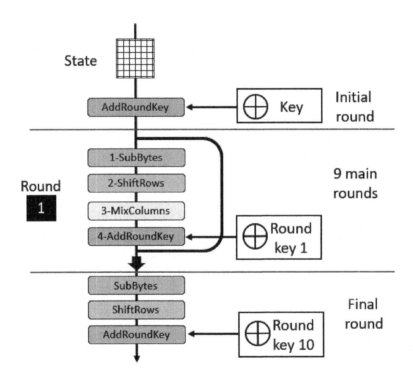

Figure 4.7 – Encrypting data with AES

The first process has the block of data in the state table going through an XOR process before going through the main rounds.

> **Important note**
>
> In some cases, you will see the first round represented as **Round 0**, which is common in computer science where programmers use a zero-based numbering system. However, when appropriate, it's easier to identify the first round as **Round 1**, as it is more user-friendly.

At the heart of the encryption process are three main transformations. Let's take a closer look at each of these, starting with substituting the bytes.

Substituting the bytes

To substitute the bytes, AES uses a **substitution box** (**S-box**), which is commonly used in a block cipher (as discussed in *Chapter 2, The Evolution of Ciphers*, under the *Entering the digital age* section). When using an S-box, each byte is substituted with the corresponding byte found in the intersection of the *x* and *y* axis, as shown in the following diagram:

43

	0	1	2	3	4	5	6	7	8	9	A	B	C	D	E	F
0	79	9A	7B	6B	9C	A4	D3	BA	72	41	7B	D0	18	94	E7	22
1	B0	7F	D7	5A	41	8B	AE	6E	5B	9E	60	82	8C	AC	33	6D
2	D5	A3	3B	B1	44	A7	4F	48	8C	FC	9B	E6	DC	6F	BE	68
3	93	79	0C	9F	22	1F	22	9C	34	CF	B6	94	A4	5D	E7	BC
4	4F	DD	AC	09	0A	98	AC	7E	D5	62	B8	13	95	AD	C4	0A
5	16	E7	68	CA	40	C7	B6	9A	6E	A2	0F	9C	7C	E8	22	EA
6	C9	A3	D2	60	7B	AC	01	7B	2E	F1	5B	CA	64	DD	42	A7
7	0A	3B	21	E1	2C	28	3E	DA	A0	2F	9C	0A	79	18	ED	77
8	68	17	8F	AC	0A	E9	F2	99	D2	8E	54	F3	31	D7	6D	8A
9	31	64	85	97	7B	CE	9B	C2	E7	A6	2A	7A	57	C3	E7	0A
A	B4	7C	13	74	FF	B0	51	F1	BB	86	A6	F4	79	0A	C9	B8
B	18	56	30	EF	BD	25	73	9F	64	47	D2	AA	CE	F3	1E	A0
C	59	91	F9	51	F1	32	7E	EE	AC	39	4F	D5	EC	94	8F	98
D	79	6D	5E	2C	0A	18	2A	3E	5C	82	A3	FA	18	8D	57	A6
E	51	47	36	3C	0A	F4	23	07	D0	7A	39	A4	2D	99	62	E0
F	0A	38	12	B9	0A	BA	47	D1	20	A7	C6	4C	1D	50	0C	E9

State Table

43	30	55	41
23	52	3B	44
41	1C	45	22
9F	33	21	0A

S-BOX

Figure 4.8 – Substituting the bytes using the S-box

In the preceding diagram, we see the first byte in the state table, **43**, will be replaced with the intersection of **4** and **3** found in the substitution box, which is **22**. The rest of the state table is substituted with the appropriate values from the S-box before moving to the next phase.

The next transformation to be carried out is to shift the rows. Let's take a look.

Shifting the rows

Shifting the rows provides permutation as well. Each byte in the state table is shifted by an appropriate number, starting with 0, as shown in the following diagram:

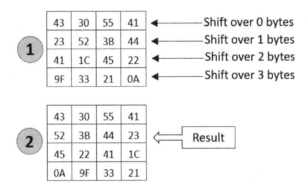

Figure 4.9 – Shifting the rows

Shifting rows works in the following manner: starting with the second row in the state table, the bytes are shifted over by 1, 2, or 3 bytes. The first row does not shift.

The resultant block of text then moves to the next phase.

The last major transformation will mix the columns. Let's see how this works, next.

Mixing the columns

Mixing the columns provides permutation of the data, as shown in the following diagram:

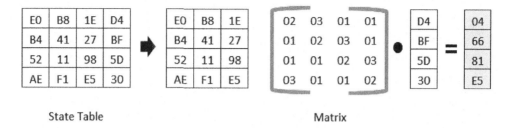

State Table   Matrix

Figure 4.10 – Mixing the columns

Starting with the state table, the rightmost column is mixed using matrix multiplication as shown, which creates new values for the state table. The process is then completed on the remaining columns, and the state table will then move to the next phase.

> **Important note**
>
> The matrix uses the values 01, 02, and 03, which are small, so that the operation can be completed quickly and provide an effective way to transform the data.

After the appropriate number of rounds, the process moves the block of data to the final phases of substituting bytes, shifting rows, and adding the round key.

AES is used in all modern applications to encrypt and secure data. However, there are other symmetric algorithms. Let's discuss a few of these, next.

Identifying other symmetric algorithms

In addition to DES and AES, scientists have developed other symmetric ciphers, such as the **International Data Encryption Algorithm (IDEA)**, **Rivest Cipher 6 (RC6)**, and Blowfish.

IDEA is a strong cipher designed to replace DES. It operates on 64-bit blocks and uses a 128-bit key, is one of the few ciphers that is patented, and requires a license for commercial use.

In addition, there are a few ciphers developed by Ron Rivest, which include the following:

- **Rivest Cipher 4 (RC4)**: This is a stream cipher used in the **Wired Equivalency Protocol (WEP)**, and then later WPA

- **RC6**: This is a block cipher that was one of the candidates for AES. RC6 is also patented and may require royalty payments for any implementation of the code.

> **Important note**
>
> We will discuss RC4 in *Chapter 10, Protecting Cryptographic Techniques*, under the *Recognizing cryptographic attacks* section. As we'll learn, the first version of RC4 was not secure. However, improvements were made in the way the algorithm was implemented, which made it more secure. As a result, RC4 was then able to be used in WPA.

Bruce Schneier is a well-known scientist who has developed several encryption algorithms. Two of Schneier's ciphers are Blowfish and Twofish, outlined as follows:

- **Blowfish** is a sleek, efficient Feistel network that encrypts 64-bit blocks. Typically, it uses a 128-bit key; however, it can employ a key up to 448 bits in length. Blowfish is free, widely used in applications such as the OpenBSD password-hashing algorithm, and encrypts data faster than DES.

- **Twofish** was one of the five finalists during the selection of AES. It encrypts data using a 128-bit block and key sizes of 128, 192, or 256 bits, and is used in many applications. To read more on where you can find Twofish, visit `https://www.schneier.com/academic/twofish/products/`.

An important element of an encryption algorithm is the key. When encrypting data, the algorithm generally takes the key and creates subkeys according to a key schedule. Let's take a look at how this works, next.

Scheduling the keys

When using symmetric encryption, the data is encrypted by an algorithm and a single shared key. Key lengths vary, but only one key is used. As we have seen, encrypting data is done with a succession of rounds. So that each round is encrypted with a specific subkey, most algorithms use a **key schedule** to generate the appropriate subkeys.

In some cases, the key schedule is very simple. For example, when using the **Tiny Encryption Algorithm (TEA)**, the key schedule simply divides the 128-bit key into four 32-bit keys to be used while encrypting data.

> **Important note**
> The TEA is a strong encryption algorithm used to secure text. To learn more,
> visit `http://www.enetplanet.com/enc/`.

However, a key schedule should be resistant to attacks. As a result, some algorithms use a more elaborate key schedule in an attempt to conceal the actual encryption key. Algorithms can vary, in that some use a one-way function and others use parts of the encryption algorithm to expand the key. Regardless of which method is used, a strong key-scheduling algorithm will reduce the ability for malicious actors to break the cipher.

For the most part, symmetric algorithms provide fast, efficient data encryption that can be accomplished using either a block or a stream cipher. Let's see what's involved in each method, next.

Dissecting block and stream ciphers

Symmetric encryption algorithms are flexible, in that they can encrypt data using a block or stream cipher. In this section, we'll compare the two and see why, in most cases, a stream cipher is the preferred method to encrypt data.

Let's start with a discussion on how a block cipher works.

Using a block cipher

A block cipher uses either a 64- or a 128-bit block of plaintext to produce a same-size block of ciphertext.

While this seems a simple way to encrypt data, we must keep in mind when using a block cipher that the block of data must be exactly the fixed-size requirement. Therefore, if encrypting data using a block size of 128 bits, the input must be 128 bits.

A block of data is rarely the exact size for a given encryption algorithm. As a result, if we need to encrypt 92 bits of data using a 128-bit block cipher, 32 bits of padding must be added. Too much padding during encryption will make the process inefficient. A better solution is to use a stream cipher, as data can be encrypted on a block of data of any size.

Next, let's investigate how stream ciphers encrypt data.

Generating a stream

Instead of encrypting data in a fixed-size block, a stream cipher encrypts 1 bit or byte at a time.

A stream cipher passes the plaintext through a pseudorandom keystream of characters, using an XOR operation.

> **Important note**
>
> The term *pseudorandom* means it appears to be random, as the character sequence is not predictable. To learn more about randomness, visit
> `https://www.random.org/`.

The characters can be any combination of letters and numbers, represented in binary form. The stream might look like this:

> 010110101110101001010100101010010101001

Figure 4.11 – Characters in a pseudorandom keystream

Stream ciphers are fast, use less code, and are a simple and efficient way to encrypt data of any size.

Regardless of whether you are using a block or a stream cipher, the data is encrypted by using a method or operating mode. Let's compare the different modes, next.

Comparing symmetric encryption operation modes

When encrypting data using symmetric encryption, an operating mode defines the way the plaintext, key, and algorithm are configured to encrypt the text. Block ciphers can encrypt a variety of block sizes, such as 64-bit, 128-bit, or 256-bit, in the following modes of operation:

- **Electronic Codebook (ECB)**
- **Cipher Block Chaining (CBC)**
- **Cipher Feedback (CFB)**
- **Output Feedback (OFB)**
- **Counter Mode (CTR)**

In this section, we'll take a look at the different modes of operation used to encrypt data. We'll start with the simplest, ECB, and then move on to CBC, CFB, and OFB, which add feedback to strengthen the encryption process. We'll then finish with a look at CTR, which provides security using parallelism, to provide a more efficient way to encrypt data.

Let's start with ECB.

Using ECB

ECB is a simple block-cipher operating mode that encrypts each block of text independently, and is illustrated in the following diagram:

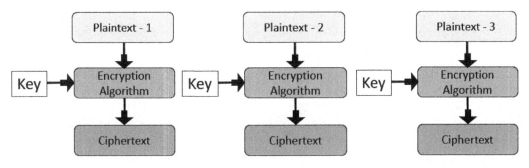

Figure 4.12 – ECB

ECB provides a fast way to encrypt data. However, this is the least secure mode, in that if there are two blocks with the same plaintext, this will result in the same ciphertext. This could then allow someone to crack the code and expose the data.

The modes outlined next will add feedback to the messages to provide additional security.

Adding feedback

With the following modes, CBC, CFB, and OFB, we'll use feedback. We'll need to start the chaining by using an **initialization vector** (**IV**), which is an encrypted block of random data used as the first 64-bit block to begin the chaining process.

With each of these, you'll see a slight change in how the data is fed into the next block of text. Let's start with CBC.

Employing CBC

This mode takes a block of plaintext and does an XOR operation with the previous block of ciphertext, and then moves on to the encryption process. To start the chain, we need to feed the first block with an IV, as shown in the following diagram:

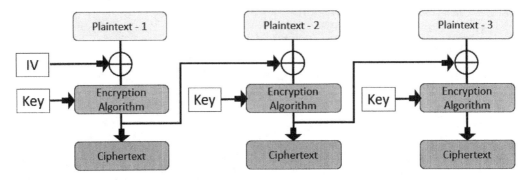

Figure 4.13 – CBC mode

The encrypted text then moves to the next block to feed into the encryption process. The next mode, CFB, also uses the encrypted text of the preceding block. Let's take a look.

Using the CFB mode

This mode is similar in design to CBC, in that we have feedback into the following block immediately after the encryption algorithm. However, the plaintext is added after the previous block and the encryption key, as shown in the following diagram:

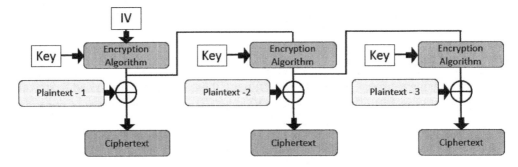

Figure 4.14 – CFB mode

The encrypted text is then XORed with the plaintext, which then outputs as ciphertext.

The next method, OFB, shifts the output so that it occurs after the data is XORed. Let's see how this works.

Understanding OFB

This mode also takes a block cipher and creates a synchronous stream cipher. With OFB, the encrypted text will feed back to the next block before it is XORed, as shown in the following diagram:

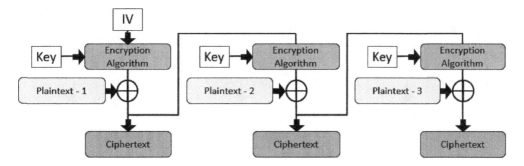

Figure 4.15 – OFB mode

The three modes CBC, CFB, and OFB each have a feedback process. The last operating mode handles data differently, as it uses a counter and a parallelized method of encrypting text. Let's see how this works, next.

Applying CTR mode

Although providing feedback strengthens the encryption process, the interconnected nature of the CBC, CFB, and OFB modes can be cumbersome. In particular, because of the fact the data is in a chain, it can be difficult to jump ahead—for example, while streaming a movie.

A better alternative is CTR, which uses the following two unique features:

- A 96-bit **number used once** (**nonce**), which is an unpredictable value
- A 32-bit counter that increments the nonce by one

Instead of an IV, the nonce and the counter are concatenated (to become a 128-bit block) and are used to feed the process, as shown in the following diagram:

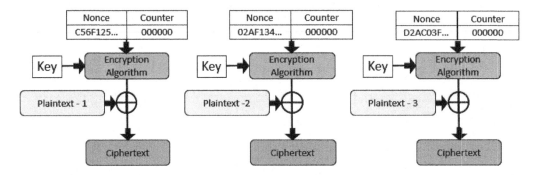

Figure 4.16 – Counter mode

While this is similar to the parallel nature of ECB, the nonce adds randomness to the encryption process.

Related to this is an improved counter mode called **Galois/Counter Mode** (**GCM**), which uses a **Galois field** (**GF**) to ensure message authentication.

Now that we understand the various operating modes, let's discuss a practical example of using symmetric encryption, in how we secure our wireless communications. Let's take a look, next.

Securing wireless communications

Wireless communication is pervasive in today's society. Also known as the 802.11 standard (Wi-Fi), this form of communication is a radio wave that can be easily attacked. Some best-practice suggestions to protect Wi-Fi traffic include the following:

- Restrict access by securing your router.
- Use antimalware protection.
- Change the default password on your device.
- Use encryption to protect the data.

In this section, we'll briefly outline why we need to encrypt our wireless traffic, and take a look at some common protocols for Wi-Fi.

Let's start with a discussion on why we need to secure our wireless communications.

Preventing eavesdropping

When sending and receiving wireless transactions on a LAN, there may be sensitive information transmitted. For example, if you are in a coffee shop that offers free internet, the connection might not be encrypted.

Using an unencrypted connection will leave your data exposed. A malicious actor might be able to obtain your information, such as credit card numbers or login credentials, by using traffic sniffing. Because of this threat, it's best to encrypt data with the strongest protocol available.

> **Important note**
>
> We discussed the concept of traffic sniffing in *Chapter 3, Evaluating Network Attacks*, under the *Comparing passive and active attacks* section.

In the next section, let's compare the different encryption protocols for wireless traffic.

Comparing protocols

Over the years, several encryption protocols have been developed to protect our wireless communications. The Wi-Fi alliance is influential in providing guidance on wireless standards and has worked to improve each iteration in the evolution of security protocols.

Let's talk about the main wireless protocols, starting with the WEP.

Exploring the Wired Equivalency Protocol

WEP is the original wireless encryption protocol. It used the RC4 stream cipher with either a 40 or 104-bit key that was static and had to be manually entered on the wireless access points. WEP used a **cyclic redundancy check (CRC)** to support data integrity.

WEP was proven to be insecure. After the inherent weaknesses of WEP became apparent, the Wi-Fi alliance immediately worked to develop a more secure protocol for wireless communications. They formed a task force to address this issue. Then, in 2004, the new identifier, IEEE 802.11i, became the designator for wireless LAN security.

> **Important note**
>
> The IEEE working group for **Wireless LANs (WLANs)** is identified as 802.11. After each new wireless protocol is ratified, you'll see it indicated by 802.11x, where x is the version.
>
> Periodically, IEEE combines standards and renames the standard. For example, in 2007, the group combined multiple 802.11 standards that included a, b, d, e, g, h, i, and j, to become IEEE 802.11-2007.

The next wireless security standard was WPA. Let's investigate this evolution, next.

Dissecting the WPA standards

WPA was designed to overcome the flaws found in WEP. Over the years, WPA has evolved to ensure improved encryption protocols for wireless communication.

Let's start with the original version, WPA.

Introducing WPA

WPA provided a stepping stone from WEP. Although WPA continued to use RC4, the algorithm employed a longer initialization vector and added a 256-bit key length.

WPA featured the **Temporal Key Integrity Protocol (TKIP)**, which dynamically generated a new 128-bit key for each packet. In addition, WPA included a **Message Integrity Check (MIC)**, which provided a stronger method (than a CRC) to ensure data integrity.

Although an improvement over WEP, WPA is not recommended. A newer version of WPA soon followed. Let's take a look.

Moving to WPA2

The next generation of WPA was WPA2, which was an improvement over WPA. Many began to implement the new standard as early as 2004. WPA2 seemed to start afresh as it replaced RC4 and TKIP with the **Counter Mode CBC-MAC Protocol (CCMP)**, using AES.

CCMP provides strong encryption and authentication. However, the standard continued to improve, with the release of WPA3 in 2018. Let's see why this is currently the most robust method to encrypt wireless traffic.

Securing Wi-Fi with WPA3

WPA3 was designed as a replacement to WPA2, and includes advanced features to secure wireless transmissions, such as the following:

- Implements 192-bit encryption when using WPA3-Enterprise mode (used in business LANs)

- Provides improved authentication

- Employs a 48-bit initialization vector

- Uses **Protected Management Frames (PMFs)** to prevent exposure of management traffic

Of all the standards, WPA3 provides the most robust security and should be used if available. For a comparison of methods to secure wireless communication, visit `https://searchnetworking.techtarget.com/feature/Wireless-encryption-basics-Understanding-WEP-WPA-and-WPA2`.

Summary

In this chapter, we began with a review of the evolution of symmetric encryption. We saw how IBM played a pivotal role in the early development of encryption, which was designed to protect consumer data. We learned how Horst Feistel and the IBM scientists designed the Feistel cipher. This then led to the development of Lucifer, which was an immediate precursor to DES.

We then discovered how symmetric encryption works, and discussed the development of DES. We saw how scientists were concerned that someone could launch a brute-force attack on DES, because of the short key. This concern led to the adoption of AES. We then dissected the main transformations of AES. In addition to DES and AES, we learned about other symmetric algorithms, along with a discussion on how subkeys are generated.

We compared the difference between block and stream ciphers and evaluated the different symmetric-encryption operating modes. We finished with a discussion on how we secure 802.11 transmissions and learned why WPA3 is currently the best encryption protocol in use today for wireless communications.

In the next chapter, we'll take a look at asymmetric (or public key) encryption, which uses two keys, a public and a private key. We'll see how using two keys solves many problems, such as securely exchanging the shared secret key that is used in symmetric encryption along with protecting our email. We'll then evaluate some of the cryptographic requirements when using asymmetric encryption and compare some algorithms. Finally, we'll discuss the concept of a digital signature, a significant use of asymmetric encryption.

Questions

Now, it's time to check your knowledge. Select the best response to the following questions and then check your answers, found in the *Assessment* section at the end of the book:

1. In the 1960s, IBM assembled a group of scientists to work on cryptography research. The team was led by scientist Horst _____, who was a recognized cryptographer.

    a. Watson

    b. Lloyd

    c. Rijndael

    d. Feistel

2. An exclusive OR of two values, 0011 and 1011, will yield_____.

    a. 1000

    b. 0010

    c. 0101

    d. 0011

3. The Feistel cipher evolved to become _____, and then later DES.

    a. Watson

    b. Lucifer

    c. Rijndael

    d. Twofish

4. A symmetric encryption algorithm uses _____.

    a. a hash value

    b. two keys that are related

    c. a single shared key

    d. two keys that are not related

5. AES encrypts data using three main transforms: substitute bytes, _____, and mix columns.

    a. invert columns

    b. exchange keysc. roll bytes

    d. shift rows

6. Bruce Schneier is a well-known scientist who has developed several encryption algorithms. Two of Schneier's ciphers are Blowfish and _____.

   a. Watson

   b. Lucifer

   c. Rijndael

   d. Twofish

7. If we need to encrypt 92 bits of data using a 128-bit block cipher, 32 bits of _____ must be added.

   a. Galois

   b. counters

   c. padding

   d. Rijndael

8. CBC, CFB, and OFB all use a logical _____ when encrypting data.

   a. AND

   b. XOR

   c. OR

   d. NOT

9. _____ uses a nonce and a counter to encrypt data.

   a. CTR

   b. CFB

   c. CBC

   d. ECB

10. _____ uses PMFs to prevent exposure of wireless management traffic.

    a. WEP

    b. WPA

    c. WPA2

    d. WPA3

Further reading

Please refer to the following links for more information:

- To read some early history on the Feistel cipher, go to `https://www.ibm.com/ibm/history/ibm100/us/en/icons/cryptography/`.

- Dive into the details of the Feistel cipher by going to `https://engineering.purdue.edu/kak/compsec/NewLectures/Lecture3.pdf`.

- Learn more about the early history of IBM by visiting `https://www.computerhistory.org/brochures/g-i/international-business-machines-corporation-ibm/`.

- For a breakdown on the DES process, visit `https://www.geeksforgeeks.org/data-encryption-standard-des-set-1/`.

- Visit `https://www.mathworks.com/help/comm/ug/working-with-galois-fields.html` to learn more about Galois fields.

- Visit `https://engineering.purdue.edu/kak/compsec/NewLectures/Lecture8.pdf` to give you more insight into AES.

- To view a comparison of stream versus block ciphers, go to `https://www.geeksforgeeks.org/difference-between-block-cipher-and-stream-cipher/`.

- If you are interested in the evolution of wireless security, visit `https://benton.pub/research/benton_wireless.pdf`.

- To learn more about the mix-columns step in AES, visit `https://www.angelfire.com/biz7/atleast/mix_columns.pdf`.

5
Dissecting Asymmetric Encryption

Symmetric algorithms offer fast, efficient encryption while ensuring data confidentiality. However, both parties must share the same secret key. In this chapter, we'll discuss the other main form of encryption: asymmetric (or public-key) encryption. We'll learn how asymmetric encryption was developed to solve the problem of securely exchanging the shared secret key, but then evolved to provide other benefits. You'll understand the two ways to obtain a shared secret key, by using encryption or using a key agreement protocol, such as Diffie-Hellman. We'll also outline how using Diffie-Hellman helps provide perfect forward secrecy.

We'll then cover other uses for public-key encryption, such as securing email and creating a digital signature. We'll discover how using standards, such as the **Public Key Cryptography Standards** (**PKCS**), helps provide interoperability among vendors. To understand what is necessary to provide a secure algorithm, we'll cover some of the cryptographic requirements for asymmetric encryption. We'll then dive into an overview of some public-key algorithms, such as **Rivest, Shamir, Adleman** (**RSA**) encryption, and **Elliptic Curve Cryptography** (**ECC**). We'll discuss how one man's passion for privacy, Phil Zimmermann, led to the development of **Pretty Good Privacy** (**PGP**). Although there is a cost involved when using PGP, we'll see how **GNU Privacy Guard** (**GPG**) can provide a free alternative. We'll finish with an overview of how digital signatures work and learn how they ensure message authenticity, integrity, and non-repudiation.

In this chapter, we're going to cover the following main topics:

- Realizing the need for asymmetric encryption
- Understanding cryptographic requirements
- Comparing public-key algorithms
- Working with digital signatures

Realizing the need for asymmetric encryption

We use symmetric encryption to secure our data transactions using a single shared secret key. When using symmetric encryption, it's best practice to change the key often to prevent it from being compromised. As a result, we need to generate and distribute the secret key securely to both parties when needed.

Because symmetric encryption uses a shared secret key, the question remains: *how do both parties securely obtain the same key?* The answer is to use a hybrid system that employs both symmetric and asymmetric encryption.

The components for asymmetric encryption, such as plaintext, ciphertext, and the encryption algorithm are similar to those used in symmetric encryption. However, instead of using the same shared key, asymmetric encryption uses two keys, a public and a private key, as shown in the following diagram:

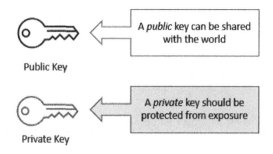

Figure 5.1 – Asymmetric key pair

The two keys are mathematically related and are generated using an asymmetric encryption algorithm, such as RSA or ECC.

In this section, we'll step through the process of exchanging the same shared key using asymmetric encryption. However, we'll also learn how Diffie-Hellman, a key agreement protocol, allows two parties to generate the same shared secret key and helps ensure perfect forward secrecy. Finally, we'll review the PKCS, which is a set of standards derived to promote interoperability among vendors.

Let's start with how we use asymmetric encryption when exchanging a shared secret key.

Securely exchanging a key

When two parties need to communicate securely across a network, such as the internet, they will generally use some form of encryption. For example, if exchanging transactional data such as the contents of a web page using **Transport Layer Security** (**TLS**), both parties will use a symmetric stream cipher. Before any data is transmitted, they will need to exchange the shared secret key that is used when encrypting data.

There are two main ways to exchange a key, outlined as follows:

- Using *encryption,* with an asymmetric algorithm, such as RSA or ECC
- Using *key agreement*, via the Diffie-Hellman process

Both parties will agree on the method to be used prior to the transaction. For example, during a TLS session, the process is determined during the handshake.

Let's take a look at each of these methods, starting with using public-key encryption.

Using public-key encryption to exchange a key

Alice and Bob need to securely communicate with one another. In order to share the secret key, they will use an asymmetric encryption algorithm.

Before beginning the process, Bob will first need to generate a key pair, and then send the public key to Alice.

To illustrate this process, we'll imagine Alice placing the shared secret key in a tennis ball. Alice will then lock the contents and send the ball over the internet to Bob, who will extract the key that is used when transacting data.

The process is shown in the following diagram:

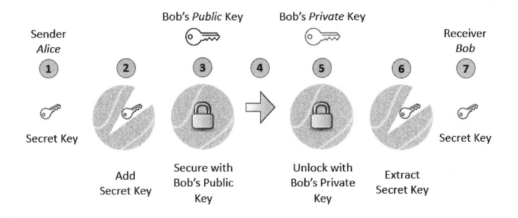

Figure 5.2 – Exchanging the shared secret key

Let's step through the process, as follows:

1.   We begin with the shared secret key on Alice's (the sender) side.

2.   The shared secret key is placed in the tennis ball.

3.   The tennis ball is encrypted using Bob's public key and the encryption algorithm.

4.   The shared secret key is sent to Bob (the recipient).

5.   The ciphertext is decrypted using Bob's private key and the decryption algorithm.

6.   The shared secret key is extracted from the tennis ball.

7.   The resultant shared secret key is presented to Bob (the receiver).

The two parties can now communicate securely using symmetric encryption.

Next, let's look at how two parties can generate a shared secret key, by using the Diffie-Hellman protocol.

Summarizing Diffie-Hellman

Mathematicians Whitfield Diffie and Martin Hellman were two scientists who worked on the development of public-key technology in the 1970s. They published the Diffie-Hellman protocol in 1976, which continues to be used in several applications today.

Unlike using asymmetric encryption to exchange a shared secret key, Diffie-Hellman is a *key agreement* protocol. The protocol is designed to have each party generate the same shared secret key (denoted by **SS** in the diagram that follows) that will be used in a session between two parties. To generate the shared secret key, there are private and public variables used in the process, as shown in the following diagram:

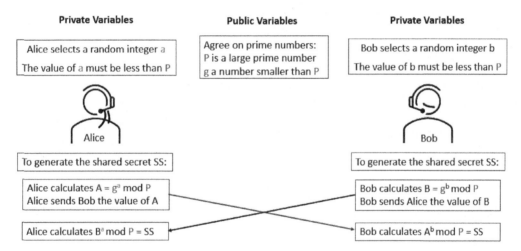

Figure 5.3 – Using the Diffie-Hellman protocol

Let's step through the process of generating a shared secret.

> **Important note**
>
> In a real-life situation, the numbers selected would be significantly larger. However, for this example, we'll use smaller numbers so that you can follow along.

To start the process, we'll need some variables.

Selecting the variables

Each party will need to select some public variables and some private variables.

Public variables

Alice and Bob first agree on two prime numbers P and g, which are not secret. These are outlined here:

- **Prime value P**: In practice, the value of P is a large prime number for security reasons. Today, it's common to see P using >2,000 bits.
- **Prime value g**: The value of the base g is small and must be less than P.

For the purpose of this example, we'll select the following public variables:

- P: 23
- g: 7

Private variables

Alice and Bob then each privately pick two random integers (a whole number), which must be less than P. These are outlined as follows:

- Alice's private integer, identified as a
- Bob's private integer, identified as b

For the purpose of this example, we'll select the following private variables:

- Alice a: 5
- Bob b: 4

Once the variables are selected, the shared secret key is calculated using the variables. The Diffie-Hellman process uses modulo arithmetic, where the modulo is the remainder after division.

Calculating the shared secret key

Using the variables, the following will generate the shared secret:

1. Alice calculates $A = g^\wedge a \bmod P$ and sends Bob the value $A = 16,807$.
2. Bob calculates $B = g^\wedge b \bmod N$ and sends Alice $B = 2,401$.
3. Alice computes $B^\wedge a \bmod P = 8$.
4. Bob computes $A^\wedge b \bmod P = 8$.

The shared secret key is 8.

Now that the two parties have the same shared secret key, both parties can use the shared secret to securely exchange data using symmetric encryption.

Using the Diffie-Hellman protocol helps ensure perfect forward secrecy. One main reason is that new keys can be generated on demand for each session, without the need to preserve a public-private key pair. This powerful feature helps improve the data-security process, as it provides assurances that no one can compromise the session keys, even if someone obtains the server's private key. We'll learn more about perfect forward secrecy in *Chapter 9, Exploring IPsec and TLS*.

It's important to understand that the Diffie-Hellman algorithm is not used for encryption; it's used so that each party generates the same shared key. To read more, visit `https://tools.ietf.org/html/rfc2631`.

Once public-key cryptography made it possible to obtain a shared secret key, scientists felt it was important to create standards, to ensure interoperability between applications. Next, let's take a look at how the PKCS helps bridge the gap among vendors and applications.

Outlining the PKCS

Once industry fully embraced public-key cryptography and began to see the potential uses across applications, the need for consistency became apparent.

In the early 1990s, RSA Security, along with several industry leaders, crafted a set of standards. If implemented, the standards would allow interoperability among various vendors.

The PKCS began with 15 standards. However, as time has passed, several have either been merged with other standards or have been deprecated and are no longer in use.

Some of the standards include the following:

- **PKCS #1** defines the rules and construct of the RSA encryption standard, which includes generating public and private keys, digital certificates, and the digital signature scheme.

- **PKCS #3** provides the methodology to use the Diffie-Hellman key agreement protocol, and specific instructions for some of the parameters in order to generate an appropriate key length.

- **PKCS #10** defines the construct of an X.509 certificate from the **certificate authority (CA)**. The certificate must include components such as the public key and distinguished name of the subject, verified with a digital signature of the CA.

> **Important note**
>
> We'll learn more about X.509 certificates in *Chapter 8, Using a Public Key Infrastructure*.

The PKCS is constantly updated to keep apace with current technologies in data security standards. When researching a standard, make sure you have the latest **Request for Comments (RFC)**.

For example, when looking at the current PKCS #1 RFC: 8017, at `https://tools.ietf.org/html/rfc8017`, in the upper-left corner you will see the following statement: `Obsoletes: 3447`.

When a new standard is written, the RFC will then indicate what the next version is by the statement `Obsoleted by: XXX`, where X indicates the next standard.

Now that we can see how we use asymmetric encryption to securely exchange a shared secret key, let's take a look at what is required when generating a public and private key pair.

Understanding cryptographic requirements

When using asymmetric encryption, we need an algorithm that can generate a mathematically related key pair. In this section, we'll take a look at some of the cryptographic requirements of using an asymmetric algorithm, and we'll see an example of generating a key pair. We'll then discuss the importance of managing the public and private key, and finish with ways we can use asymmetric encryption.

Let's start with some requirements when generating a key pair.

Designing a strong algorithm

When something is strong it is resistant to being broken, such as an impenetrable fortress. An encryption algorithm is no exception, in that we want one that is able to withstand a brute-force attack and continue to provide data confidentiality and integrity. Some of the considerations when designing a strong asymmetric algorithm include the following:

- It must be effortless to generate a mathematically related public and private key pair.

- Even with knowledge of the public key, it is infeasible to determine the private key.

- Even with knowledge of the public key, it is infeasible to determine the plaintext without the private key.

- Either key can be used for encryption, with the other used for decryption and vice versa.

Now that you understand the parameters of a strong algorithm, let's see an example of generating a key pair.

Generating a key pair

There are several apps that you can use to generate a key pair. However, so that you can see what a public and private key actually looks like, we'll generate a key pair using PGP on the *iGolder* website. If you would like to follow along, go to `https://www.igolder.com/pgp/`.

Once at the *iGolder* website you will see some choices, such as the **PGP Key Generator**, along with the **PGP Encryption Tool** and **PGP Decryption Tool**.

For this exercise, select the **PGP Key Generator**. On that page, you will need to add some variables to create your key pair, as follows:

- **Email Address**: Enter a fictitious email address, as this will not affect the process. For this exercise, we'll use `Roxy@Kiddikatz.com`.

- **PGP-Key Password / Passphrase**: Enter a fictitious passphrase. For this exercise, we'll use `orangetigerkittens`.

Once the two variables are entered, select **Generate PGP keys**. You will then see your private and public key pair. The following is the public key that you would share with everyone:

```
-----BEGIN PGP PUBLIC KEY BLOCK-----
Version: BCPG C# v1.6.1.0

mQENBGAF6Y8BCAC5FBW5nqat8bY/ThjjJ/T6o1rJzbM8zT47YqYQ/ga9ui+RH/
0yOeTdJn4aoB1oBpOrRz6g12b39JxB5ZA+AoD7WtgvZN5NjOjGxfY0J6PTPJBz
VR8gFZMto4jni7Ciflex/9Vc6zeDA7v/Up9TcDeetMrO18HxF06QO55u8dT
pwuq0ZOWSwfCNS31MHAcOtInE7Mg7iKIMGeEOPKYWhCNcmxdi05ImWZo7vl
MgLWPge1daYkcWZAyw7kB9hZ63Mt4GEBKibhyE4enV2zboHkhYfB9YoZm2w
CiXkjAViQ4GWjc+XytgQtZS16NASbI6KuGgZHJeeCFaJDNZG6iyWyClABEB
AAG0E1JveH1AS21kZG1rYXR6LmNvbYkBHAQQAQIABgUCYAXpjwAKCRCHxe7
CK11VqzC2CACeXgEZo1SQR4C4HvbvzvRqkQQ/T/RBrNy4Ct1Dh1EVzfeu7
mdsnMakP28iktbnjdPIIamgUjbNUvjzgj/qACvvDEPmjHe+B7nqkMi+1VNP
1TuJnZWKMW2j3yTEx8Wie4WFSeWPF0i/7j/0UrzBPggk8TGons4fkrkZCi6
```

pKucpekXdl5F9Zqre16PTHXwTcgIbj/kH3A9D6SdnEHVb6XxPRnLp4FxAmLAOt
DBZu0XYvkk0fCigy2nWwSpgCiPscOmu0pmlpeydfWVgDVv6hLmSzZscODCOjXa
5nT63HDN6bRzKm2LNbefnd0EkC8y0H6HMpvs+7jX6VMtMm6Vn
2UTQ
=aF8z
-----END PGP PUBLIC KEY BLOCK-----

If you want to use the key pair to encrypt text, you will need to save it to your system. The *iGolder* website also has a location that you can use to encrypt a block of text, by going to `https://www.igolder.com/pgp/encryption/`.

As you can see, it's easy to generate a key pair and encrypt data. But what about saving and sharing your two keys? Managing keys is another important concept when dealing with asymmetric encryption.

Let's explore this concept, next.

Managing keys

One important concept in asymmetric encryption is that you have two keys. As outlined earlier, the following applies:

- A *public* key is public for everyone to see.
- A *private* key must be kept private.

For transactions on the web, key management is done by your operating system. For other purposes, such as using GPG email security or managing cryptocurrency in a Bitcoin wallet, it may be up to the individual to manage the keys.

Let's discuss some concepts when storing a private key.

Storing a private key

An individual should protect their private key from exposure or compromise. If someone's key is lost or stolen there can be serious consequences, such as the following:

- The individual won't be able to decrypt email messages that use a public-key encryption application, such as PGP.
- A malicious party may be able to access their data or, in some cases, the contents of a crypto wallet.

As a result, any private keys need to be securely stored. One option is to use a dedicated device, such as a **Universal Serial Bus (USB)** token. Another option is to store the key on a smart card and secure the card using a biometric, such as a fingerprint.

As opposed to a private key, which must be kept private, when using asymmetric encryption we freely share our public key with everyone. Let's outline what options we have for distributing, publishing, and storing a public key.

Publishing a public key

Public keys are designed so that anyone can obtain them. You can store your key on a key server, send via email, or even post on a blog or website. For example, Phil Zimmermann, the creator of PGP, posts his public keys here:

```
https://philzimmermann.com/text/PRZ_keys.txt
```

Sharing keys is easy; however, trusting that the keys are authentic is another concern. We'll explore the issue of trust later in this chapter, in the *Trusting public keys* section.

Let's cover some uses for asymmetric encryption.

Using asymmetric encryption

Scientists realized soon after the development of asymmetric encryption that having a pair of keys to work with is powerful. Over the years, symmetric encryption has evolved to be used in several different ways, including the following:

- Exchanging the shared secret key
- Securing our email
- Producing a blockchain
- Creating digital signatures

When we think about asymmetric encryption, we see that we can use it for many different applications. However, we do not use symmetric encryption to send and receive data across a network. The reason is that asymmetric encryption is not that efficient.

Some asymmetric algorithms have long key lengths—for example, RSA can use a key between 1,024 and 4,096 bits. Many feel the longer key length has an impact on processing when encrypting and decrypting data.

In addition, asymmetric encryption is resource-intensive as compared to symmetric encryption, which generally uses basic operations such as an **exclusive OR (XOR)** or a left circular shift. In contrast, asymmetric encryption uses multiplication and division, and can take up to 1,000 times as long to perform as symmetric encryption.

That is why most encryption systems are hybrid, using both symmetric and asymmetric encryption.

By now, you can see the value of using asymmetric encryption. Next, let's take a look at some public-key algorithms.

Comparing public-key algorithms

We understand what is required to create a strong algorithm and see the value in using a key pair. In this section, we'll take a look at a few public-key algorithms, such as RSA and ECC. We'll also see how PGP and GPG can secure our email with little or no effort. Finally, we'll discuss methods we use to ensure trust when using a public key.

Let's start with outlining how RSA is used to secure data.

Outlining RSA

In 1977, Ron Rivest, Adi Shamir, and Len Adleman developed RSA, a widely recognized cipher that is used in a number of different applications.

RSA uses a variety of encryption key lengths that include the following: 1,024-bit, 2,048-bit, and 4,096-bit lengths. The algorithm is used when sending a shared secret key in symmetric encryption. However, it can also be used to encrypt documents and create a digital signature.

Let's step through what is involved when calculating private and public keys using RSA.

Calculating the keys

We'll take a look at the RSA formula that is used to calculate our keys.

In the first step, the algorithm selects two large prime numbers, as follows:

- **Prime value**: P
- **Prime value**: g

Calculate N by multiplying the two primes, as follows:

- $N = P^*g$

Compute the (Euler) totient of N, which is the following:

- $\emptyset(N) = (P\text{-}1) * (g\text{-}1)$

> **Important note**
>
> If p and q are two primes, the Euler totient of $p*g$ is this value: $(p\text{-}1) * (g\text{-}1)$.

Select e (public key) so that it is > coprime (or mutually prime) to $\emptyset(N)$, $e > 1$ coprime to $\emptyset(N)$.

Select d (private key) so that $de\ mod\ \emptyset(N) = 1$.

> **Important note**
>
> When selecting d, the algorithm will verify the value. This is done by multiplying the public key by the private key and dividing the product by the Euler totient, to ensure that there is a remainder of 1.

Now that we see the formula, let's calculate our keys using actual values, as follows:

- *Prime value P: 167*
- *Prime value g: 173*
- *$N = P*g = 28,891$*
- *Euler totient of $N = 28,552$*
- *Select e (public key) = 23*
- *Select d (private key) = 6207*

RSA is considered to be a secure algorithm. This is due to the fact that it is exceedingly difficult to break the encryption, as it requires being able to factor large prime numbers to obtain the key. It remains a solid algorithm that is widely used; however, another alternative is ECC. Let's see what's involved when using ECC, next.

Visualizing an elliptical curve

An elliptical curve is a mathematical function using the formula $y^2 = x^3 + ax + b$, where x and y are integers within a field. The *parameters* of the curve are a and b. When graphed in a standard two-dimensional x, y coordinate system, the values of a and b will create curves, as shown in the following screenshot:

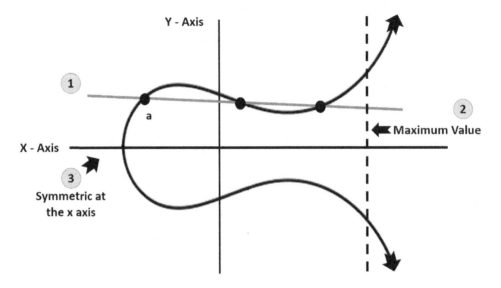

Figure 5.4 – An elliptical curve

In the preceding screenshot, we see a few key elements, as follows:

- If you draw a line, it will intersect the curve in no more than three points.
- When dealing with ECC, everything is kept within the finite field (or maximum value), which represents the key size.
- An elliptical curve is symmetric at the x axis.

> **Important note**
> The shape of the curve will change, depending on the value of a and b. For an online elliptical curve generator, go to https://www.desmos.com/calculator/ialhd71we3.

Because of the symmetric nature of an elliptical curve, any point on one side will be equal to the other side. As shown in the following screenshot, b and c, along with d and e, are opposite one another:

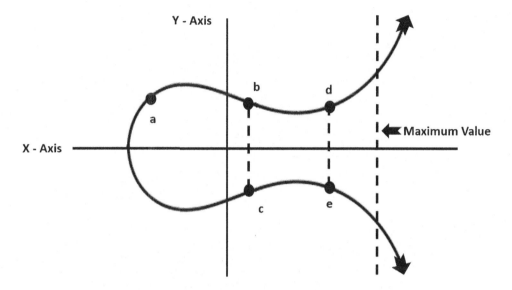

Figure 5.5 – The symmetric nature of an elliptical curve

Each point represents a coordinate on the graph. We will use these points, as the dominant operation in ECC cryptographic schemes is point multiplication. Let's take a look at how this works.

Connecting the dots

As illustrated, within the curve there are multiple points, such as b, c, d, and e. In a large elliptical curve, there will be many more points.

To begin, we'll need a starting point a (or generator), which will generate the value that will represent the private key. The generator will connect to another point (called dotting) and can be repeated multiple times. The algorithm will connect the generator (shown as a) with various points within the graph.

In the following screenshot, we see how *a -> b*, *a -> c*, and *a -> d*:

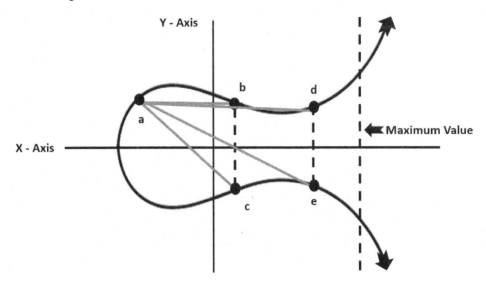

Figure 5.6 – Dotting the coordinates

You can connect point *a* with any other points that exist in the graph any number of times; however, the connections must remain within the limit of the maximum value.

The private key in an ECC is the number of times (*n*) you dot the generator *a* with another point on the graph.

Because the maximum value represents the size of the key, if you increase the key size you will expand the space you are able to work with. An expanded space will increase the number of values and decrease the ability of anyone figuring out the private key.

Even with knowledge of where *a* resides, along with the function that created the graph, it's extremely difficult to find out the number for the private key. ECC is nearly impossible to crack because of the sheer number of possible points on the curve. As a result, ECC is a strong algorithm, as discussed next.

Offering a strong algorithm

ECC has been around since 1985, when mathematicians Neal Koblitz and Victor S. Miller outlined the use of using curves to encrypt data. However, ECC didn't really become a recognized algorithm for encryption until 2004.

Scientists have discovered that ECC has several benefits, one of which is that it can use a significantly smaller key size. As opposed to RSA, which can use a key length of up to 4096 bits, using a 384-bit key with ECC is felt to be exceptionally strong.

The smaller key translates into more efficiency and less storage needed overall. When the ECC is used in TLS certificates, it decreases the time it takes to perform handshakes. Ultimately, this can reduce processing, help websites load faster, and decrease bandwidth requirements.

Because of this efficiency, ECC is ideal for devices with a small form factor and limited processing and storage, such as mobile devices, **Internet of Things (IoT)**, and smart cards.

ECC is a complex method to secure data and is gaining momentum, as it uses a much smaller key while providing robust security.

Now that we understand some of the asymmetric encryption algorithms, let's take a look at an application using public-key encryption, which is designed to secure our email.

Providing PGP

Over the years, there have been many laws written that require vendors to provide a method for government and law enforcement to gain access to encrypted data. Methods include building a backdoor or providing a decryption tool. In 1991, the US government developed several laws to allow access to encrypted data. In response, Phil Zimmermann, a technology leader and visionary, developed PGP so that individuals could control who is able to see their information.

PGP is an asymmetric encryption algorithm used to encrypt and secure emails and documents. PGP provides all the functions of an asymmetric encryption algorithm: key exchange, encryption, and digital signatures. When using PGP with an email client, it is transparent to the user. As long as both parties have exchanged their public keys, they can easily encrypt a message with a public key when sending an email, and the recipient can decrypt the message with their private key.

Stepping through the process

Alice needs to securely send a document to Bob. To accomplish this, Alice and Bob will use PGP encryption to secure the message, as shown in the following diagram:

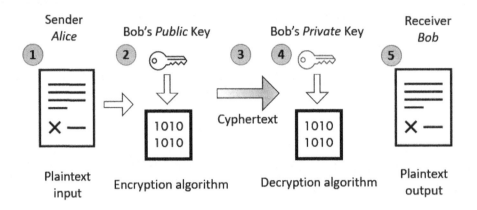

Figure 5.7 – Encrypting mail using PGP

Let's step through the process, as follows:

1. We begin with the plaintext (data) input on Alice's (the sender) side.

2. The plaintext is encrypted using Bob's public key and the encryption algorithm.

3. The ciphertext is sent to Bob (the recipient).

4. The ciphertext is decrypted using Bob's private key and the decryption algorithm.

5. The resultant plaintext (or data) is presented to Bob (the receiver).

Originally, PGP was freely available; however, it is now a commercial product. There are alternatives, including the following:

- OpenPGP, which was developed to be similar in nature to PGP and can be found here:

  `https://www.openpgp.org/`

- GPG is also derived from the PGP standard and is found here:

  `https://gnupg.org/`

Each of these can be used to secure your email. GPG includes applications such as Claws, a lightweight email client, so that you can start using GPG to securely send and receive emails.

When working with software such as PGP and GPG, you will generate a public and private key pair. You'll need to share your public key with someone else, as that will be used when sending and receiving emails.

A malicious actor can present another entity's key and spoof someone into thinking it belongs to someone else. We must be aware of this and understand that the one main concern when using a public key is the level of trust we assign in the key. Let's discuss this, next.

Trusting public keys

Once created, a public key isn't automatically authenticated, and no one really knows if a public key belongs to the person specified. Consequently, users must verify that their public keys belong to them.

As outlined, a public key is made available to everyone. However, there is no native way that you can be sure that the key belongs to the individual that has sent the key to you or shared it to a key server.

As a result, an important concept we must address while communicating with entities on the internet and dealing with public keys is the issue of trust. There are two ways to address trust: the **Web of Trust** and **certificates**.

Let's take a look at using the Web of Trust when using a public key.

Using the Web of Trust

Phil Zimmerman introduced the Web of Trust after developing PGP. The method is this: instead of a CA such as Go Daddy to decide whether or not a public key can be trusted, we look to a trusted introducer.

We will use this example: You work in the payroll department. Your manager tells everyone that your department is now going to use GPG for email communications. Once the software is installed, everyone creates their own key pair and sends their public key to the manager. The manager will then assign trust.

Generally, a public key will have one of the following levels of trust:

- **Unknown**: Keys start at this level. It's up to someone to change this, depending on how comfortable they are in assigning a higher level of trust.

- **None**: Don't trust this key as the owner has not signed keys correctly in the past.

- **Marginal**: Set for people that you know remotely, perhaps a close acquaintance.

- **Full**: You can trust this key, usually your own or someone you saw create the key.

The Web of Trust works in signing public keys in an intimate environment, but on a larger, untrusted environment we need another option. Let's discuss using certificates to assure trust during a transaction on the internet.

Employing certificates to provide trust

On the internet, we use the **Public Key Infrastructure** (**PKI**). In the PKI, the CA generates a digital certificate to securely distribute keys between a server (such as a web server) and a client. The signed certificate ensures the authentication of each entity in a digital transaction. We'll learn more about the PKI in *Chapter 8, Using a Public Key Infrastructure*.

As we have seen, there are a few common asymmetric encryption algorithms, and these include RSA, Diffie-Hellman, and ECC. There are also a few others. We'll most likely see the development of additional asymmetric algorithms in the next few years, to meet the needs of our ever-changing technology landscape.

As we have learned, there are several uses for asymmetric encryption, and that includes creating a digital signature. Let's take a look.

Working with digital signatures

A digital signature is a cryptographic technique that uses asymmetric encryption to provide several services for both sender and receiver. Instead of encrypting an entire document, a digital signature encrypts only a hash of the message, therefore using a smaller footprint.

In this section, we'll see how a digital signature can ensure message authentication, integrity, and non-repudiation. Then, we'll step through the process so that you can see how all of these are accomplished when creating a signature.

Let's start with how we can provide three core security services.

Providing core security services

Because of the vast anonymous nature of the internet, many felt that there needed to be a way of creating and signing a document, using a digital format. The method was to address the issue of being able to complete transactions on the internet without requiring a physical or wet signature, whereby someone physically marks a document.

In 2000, the US government signed into law the **Electronic Signatures in Global and National Commerce (ESIGN) Act**, which legalized the use of digital signatures on documents. The concept of a digital signature solves several issues. One is that it provides message authentication. Let's discuss this, next.

Ensuring authentication

When dealing with an entity on the internet, it's especially important to guarantee authenticity as this assures both parties that the message originated from an authorized source.

A digital signature assures authentication by using a **Hashed Message Authentication Code (HMAC)**. To create a HMAC, we use a secure hash function (such as SHA-256) that takes a variable length input and creates a fixed-length output. This hash (also called a **message digest**) is then encrypted using the private key of the sender, to produce a digital signature.

Once the receiver obtains the message, the HMAC is decrypted using the sender's public key. This verifies that the message came from the sender and not an imposter.

Another service that is paramount is that of message integrity. Let's see how this is accomplished.

Guaranteeing integrity

Providing message integrity ensures that data is not modified, lost, or destroyed in either an accidental or unauthorized manner. A HMAC not only provides message authentication but is also used to ensure data integrity.

Prior to signing the message, a hash of the document is generated and then attached to the message. Once the receiver obtains the message, a new hash of the document is generated and then compared to the one attached to the message. If they are the same, this will verify that the message was not modified in any way.

One other service that a digital signature provides is non-repudiation. Let's review this concept.

Assuring non-repudiation

When two people are completing a transaction on the internet, it could be fairly easy to spoof an email or claim that you did not send a message.

The concept of non-repudiation prevents a party from denying participation in a communication. By using a digital signature, the sender must sign the message with their private key. This action ensures non-repudiation as the signature will provide proof that the message was sent by a specific entity.

Now that we have seen which services we can provide using a digital signature, let's see what's involved when generating one.

Creating a digital signature

To create a digital signature, the sender will use their private key, as shown in the following diagram:

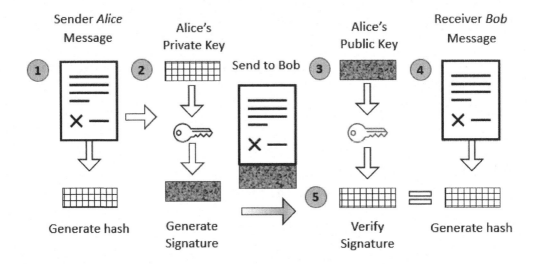

Figure 5.8 – Using a digital signature

Let's step through the process, as follows:

1. We begin with the message on Alice's (the sender) side.

2. The algorithm generates a hash of the message.

3. The hash is encrypted using Alice's private key and the encryption algorithm.

4. The message is sent to Bob (the recipient).

5. The hash is removed and is decrypted using Alice's public key and the decryption algorithm, which assures message authentication.

6.   The algorithm generates a hash of the message.

7.   The two hash values are compared. If they match, we are assured there has been no violation in integrity.

A digital signature can provide assurance of authentication and integrity and prevent non-repudiation, but with a much smaller footprint than when encrypting an entire message.

Summary

In this chapter, we saw how asymmetric encryption solved the problem of securely sharing a secret key in a data transaction. We compared two methods to achieve this, by using encryption or Diffie-Hellman, a key agreement protocol. We also saw how standards such as the PKCS assure vendor interoperability.

By now, you understand some of the requirements needed to create a strong algorithm, along with the importance of effectively managing both public and private keys. We saw the many uses for asymmetric encryption, which include key exchange, securing our email, generating a blockchain, and creating digital signatures.

We then compared a few asymmetric algorithms, such as RSA, PGP, and ECC. We also recognized that there are two main methods to provide trust when using a public key. The two ways to assure trust are the CA in a large environment such as the internet, or the Web of Trust in a smaller environment, such as an office. Finally, we saw how public-key encryption is used to create a digital signature, which assures authentication, integrity, and non-repudiation.

In the next chapter, you'll learn how a hash algorithm is a one-way function that takes a variable-length input and produces a fixed-length output. We'll identify some of the optimal hash properties. We'll then review a few common hash algorithms that are in use today and discuss how they ensure integrity. Finally, you'll learn how a message digest is created to provide message authentication, along with the steps taken to ensure this goal.

Questions

Now, it's time to check your knowledge. Select the best response to the following questions and then check your answers, found in the *Assessment* section at the end of the book:

1. _____is a key agreement protocol, designed to have each party generate the same shared secret key that will be used in the session.

    a. PGP

    b. Diffie-Hellman

    c. GPG

    d. Rivest, Shamir, Adleman

2. PKCS _____defines the construct of an X.509 certificate from the CA, and includes components such as a public key, a distinguished name, and a digital signature of the CA.

    a. #1

    b. #5

    c. #7

    d. #10

3. _____ uses a variety of encryption key lengths that include 1,024-bit, 2,048-bit, and 4,096-bit lengths.

    a. DES

    b. ECC

    c. RSA

    d. AES

4. Most encryption systems are _____ and use both symmetric and asymmetric encryption.

    a. hybrid

    b. ElGamal

    c. public

    d. elliptical

5. The dominant operation in ECC cryptographic schemes is _____ multiplication.

   a. Diffie

   b. ElGamal

   c. point

   d. certificate

6. The _____ works when assigning public keys a level of trust in an intimate environment.

   a. ocean of authentication

   b. ElGamal

   c. dotted system

   d. Web of Trust

7. A digital signature assures authentication by using a(n) _____.

   a. dotted system

   b. HMAC

   c. RSA chip

   d. elliptical chip

Further reading

Please refer to the following links for more information:

- To view a list of the PKCS, visit `https://www.educba.com/pkcs/`.

- For *Guideline for Using Cryptographic Standards in the Federal Government: Cryptographic Mechanisms*, visit `https://nvlpubs.nist.gov/nistpubs/SpecialPublications/NIST.SP.800-175b.pdf`.

- Read about RSA here: `https://gonitsora.com/rsa-elegant-code/`

- To learn more about Phil Zimmermann, you can visit `https://philzimmermann.com/EN/background/index.html`.

- To view a primer on ECC go to: `https://arstechnica.com/information-technology/2013/10/a-relatively-easy-to-understand-primer-on-elliptic-curve-cryptography/2/`.

6
Examining Hash Algorithms

If you look up the word "hash," you will see several definitions. One of the definitions is to chop food into small pieces. That is what a hash algorithm does to data. A hash algorithm will chop or reduce a variable-length block of text to produce a fixed-length hash value. The other key factor is that a hash value is a one-way function in that it cannot be restored to the original message. In this chapter, we'll describe the concept of the hash algorithm and investigate the many ways we can use a hash value.

Not all hash algorithms are the same in that some have more desirable attributes. We'll talk about what comprises an exceptional attribute when using a hash algorithm and list several desired qualities. We'll then take a look at the hash algorithms that are in use today, and why some are no longer in use. Finally, we'll take a closer look at how message authentication works, along with outlining a few practical examples.

In this chapter, we're going to cover the following main topics:

- Describing a hash algorithm
- Identifying optimal hash properties
- Comparing common hash algorithms in use today
- Authenticating a message

Describing a hash algorithm

In order to securely exchange data, we use more than just encryption algorithms, we also use cryptographic tools, techniques, and protocols.

Symmetric and asymmetric encryption ensures confidentiality by scrambling data into an unreadable form. The message won't mean anything to anyone unless they have the key. With the key, we can decrypt the data so that it makes sense.

Along with encryption, another important cryptographic technique is hashing. In this section, we'll outline what it means to create a hash of a message, and see what characteristics make a hash of a message different from encrypting a message. We'll also review the many uses for a hash algorithm.

Let's start with learning how a hash is created.

Creating a hash

Encryption uses a key or pair of keys. When we encrypt a message, we can decrypt the message as long as we have the key. A hash is different in that it is one-way. You cannot generate the original message from the hash.

A hash algorithm takes a given input of any size of data and produces a fixed-length output. When generating a hash, we create a message digest. The message digest is a fingerprint that uniquely identifies the data and assures data integrity, as *any* change to the document will change the value.

We use a hash in a number of different applications, including authenticating a message, monitoring data integrity, and storing passwords. In addition, hashing is also used in applications such as **Internet Protocol Security** (**IPsec**) to ensure data integrity and authenticity.

As discussed, a hash is a one-way function. But just what is meant by the term one-way? Let's explore this concept next.

Defining one-way

The concept of one-way when generating a hash means that no matter what method is used, you cannot generate the original message from the hash.

As shown in the graphic, a hash can take a message of any size and generate a fixed-sized message digest:

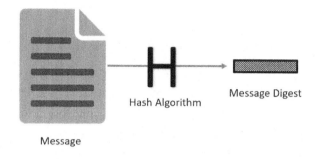

Figure 6.1 – Generating a message digest

The message digest will generally be smaller than the original message. The output size will depend on the algorithm. For example, if we compare the output of the various choices of the **Secure Hash Algorithm (SHA)** and Whirlpool, we see the output can vary:

Hash Algorithm	Message Digest Output in Bits
SHA-2 (256)	256
SHA-2 (384)	384
SHA-2 (512)	512
Whirlpool	512

Figure 6.2 – Output of various hash algorithms

> **Important note**
> When you see the terms SHA-2 (256) and SHA256, they refer to the same thing.

The small size of the message digest is optimal, as it doesn't require a huge amount of overhead to provide message integrity. For example, we reviewed Tripwire in *Chapter 1, Protecting Data in Motion or at Rest*, in the *Understanding security services* section. We saw how the software monitored data integrity by creating hash values of files stored on the system. Tripwire then compared the hash values to ensure the files were not modified.

The software only needs to store the message digest, as it is a succinct value.

But what does a message digest look like? Let's take a look.

Producing a hash

We can use a variety of algorithms to generate a hash. We saw what a **Message Digest 4 (MD4)** hash looks like in *Chapter 10, Protecting Cryptographic Techniques*, in the *Comparing various attacks* section. Now let's see what SHA256 looks like when we hash a large block of text.

To follow along, go to `https://passwordsgenerator.net/sha256-hash-generator/` and enter some data. For this example, I used this block of text:

```
Industry continued to develop desktops, laptops, games,
mobile devices, and Internet of Things that began to collect
and exchange more and more data. Concurrently, businesses,
universities, governments, and consumers began to invest
heavily in information technology, spending billions on
hardware and software designed to improve the quality of life.
```

This will output the following hash:

```
D4E65F55D777E2169A67718330C3E8C4F2BE9F692A19DCC94F84BA011
F8CF3AF
```

But what if I use a shorter phrase:

```
Orange tiger kittens
```

This will result in the following hash:

```
A24964E7F5652E89221714ACFB5C261B2036E74039B4DF2426601DC890
C4FC74
```

The point is, the length of the message doesn't matter; a hash value will always return a fixed size output. The output will depend on the algorithm. In the case of SHA-2 (256), this generates a 256-bit output.

> **Important note**
> In each of the two hash values, you will count 64 characters. That is because it's common to display the output in hexadecimal notation.

Now that we see what a hash looks like, let's see some of the many cryptographic applications for a hash algorithm.

Employing a hash function

Over the years, the hash algorithm has proven to be a valuable cryptographic asset and has found a home in many different applications. In this section, we'll list the different uses for hash algorithms.

Let's start with how a hash can ensure the integrity of a file.

Verifying file integrity

To ensure integrity for files that are downloaded from the internet, or sent to you via email, you can verify the hash value to ensure there have been no unauthorized changes. For example, if we want to download a copy of Kali Linux, we will go to `https://www.kali.org/downloads/` and select an image to download.

Once there, you will see a list of images and, alongside the image, the SHA256 value as shown here:

Image Name	Torrent	Version	Size	SHA256Sum
Kali Linux 64-Bit (Installer)	Torrent	2020.4	41.G	50492d761e400c2b5e22c8f253dd6f75c27e4bc84e33c2eff272476a0588fb02

Figure 6.3 – Kali Linux hash value

You can easily run a checksum on any file. If you don't have an app installed to calculate a checksum you can go to `https://www.7-zip.org/` and download and install 7-Zip. 7-Zip uses two checksum options:

- **Cyclic Redundancy Check (CRC)**
- **Secure Hash Algorithm (SHA)**

Once 7-Zip is installed, place your cursor over a file and then right-click and select **CRC SHA**, as shown here:

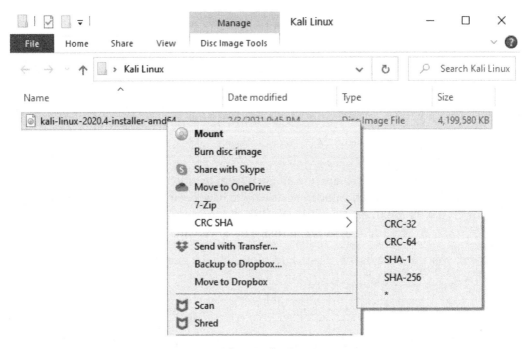

Figure 6.4 – Selecting the CRC SHA option

I selected the Kali Linux ISO and used the **SHA256** option, as shown in the following screenshot:

Figure 6.5 – The SHA 256 value for Kali Linux

The SHA 256 values match, so I am confident the image has not been modified.

In addition to ensuring file integrity, we use a hash value during the creation of a digital signature.

Creating a digital signature

If you recall the *Creating a digital signature* section of *Chapter 5, Dissecting Asymmetric Encryption*, a hash value is an integral part of the digital signature process. The process begins by generating a hash of the sender's message. The message digest is then encrypted using the sender's private key, which then becomes a **Hashed Message Authentication Code (HMAC)**. The HMAC is attached to the message and then sent to the recipient.

The recipient removes the HMAC and decrypts the value using the sender's public key and the decryption algorithm, which assures message authentication. The algorithm will then generate a hash of the original message and compare the newly created hash and the decrypted HMAC. If they match, we are assured there has been no violation in integrity.

Using an HMAC in a digital signature is efficient and results in a smaller footprint when sending messages, while also providing message authentication, integrity, and non-repudiation.

We also use a hash value when using passwords. Let's see how this works.

Verifying a password

When using an app for the first time, you'll generally create your username and password. The app will then store your username. However, instead of storing your password, the system will store a *hash* of the password. This is so that if anyone were to get hold of the password files, they would only have a list of hash values, and not the actual passwords.

Let's step through how this works. If Bob were to authenticate into a system, he will provide his username and password. His password is then converted to a hash value, and then that value is compared to the value that is stored on the server:

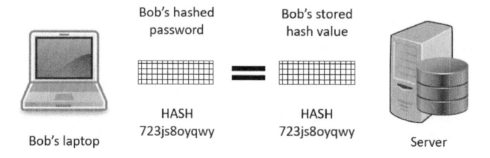

Figure 6.6 – Comparing hash values

If the hash values match, Bob will be able to gain access to the system.

Next, let's see how a hash value can help locate records in a file.

Identifying data

When dealing with a large amount of data, one way we can search for specific records is by using a hash table, as shown in the following diagram:

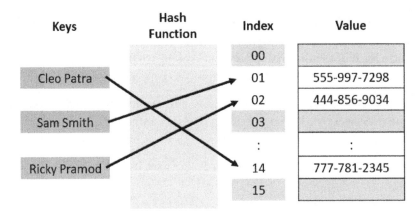

Figure 6.7 – A hash table for a phone book

A hash table is a container that maps keys to values.

This works by running a hash function on the keys (or data), and that becomes the unique index for the associated value.

Using a hash table (also known as a hash map) provides improved lookup speeds when dealing with a large amount of data, such as files on a peer-to-peer network or a genealogy database.

In addition, a hash table is used when dealing with big data.

Generating big data

Today, there are billions of devices on the **Internet of Things** (**IoT**). All of the devices are talking to us and to each other, and all of this activity generates a massive amount of data.

The data generated by IoT devices is called big data. To harness the data for practical purposes, you need to use a non-relational database, such as MongoDB. MongoDB processes data in a distributed manner using many machines. When dealing with big data, MongoDB uses hash tables to parse through the massive data stores, which helps speed up the search.

> **Important note**
>
> A classic database (such as MySQL) is a collection of records and is relational in that the database comprises tables that are related to one another. To search the database, you use **Structured Query Language** (**SQL**). On the other hand, a non-relational database stores data in the most efficient manner possible, such as key-value pairs, document storage, wide-column using tables rows and columns, or graph storage.

Another use for a hash value is in a blockchain. Let's take a look.

Creating a blockchain

Blockchain is a distributed ledger technology that has been around since 2009. Many are familiar with its use in mining Bitcoin. However, that is only one of many uses for blockchain. The technology is used in many different industries, including supply chain management, entertainment, and real-estate transactions.

Using a hash in a blockchain will chain the blocks together. This chaining makes the blockchain immutable, or unalterable. In addition, the hash is then used to search for a transaction by using a hash table.

Another use of a hash value is to provide message authentication.

Ensuring message authentication

Message integrity is another key use of a hash value. For example, when network devices communicate with one another across the network, they share information. As shown in the following diagram, we have two devices attempting to send an update to **Router B**:

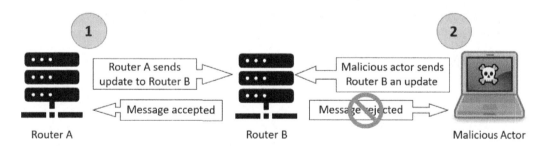

Figure 6.8 – Updates using a MAC

Using a **Message Authentication Code (MAC)**, will result in the following outcome:

1. **Router A** sends an update that is verified using a MAC. **Router B** will accept the message, as the MAC proves that the update is from an authorized device.

2. The **Malicious Actor** sends an update that does not use message authentication. Because the router cannot be sure the **Malicious Actor** is an authorized network device, the message is rejected.

Now that we see how a hash is created, along with reviewing the many uses for a hash algorithm, let's learn what makes an ideal hash algorithm.

Identifying optimal hash properties

In order for a hash algorithm to be effective, it must be able to generate a hash algorithm quickly and efficiently. In addition, it must have several other properties to provide the best security. An optimal algorithm must be able to stand the test of time and remain a solid algorithm, even with advances in technology.

In this section, we'll outline and explain some of the desired properties of an exceptional hash algorithm, such as non-reversibility, collision resistance, and determinism.

Let's start with the non-reversibility or one-way property.

Generating a one-way function

When we say one-way, we mean it. A variable-length block of data goes into the function, and a fixed-length hash is returned as the output. The output has no resemblance to the original block of data in any way. Nor is there any way to reconstruct the data to become the original. This non-reversible property is optimal as it makes a more secure hash algorithm.

Another property is that the algorithm must produce a fixed-size output.

Producing a fixed-size output

As we saw in the *Describing a hash algorithm* section, it doesn't matter what the size of the input is, a hash algorithm will always produce the same size hash. The output will depend on the given algorithm and can vary. For example, a **cyclic redundancy check (CRC)** is a type of hash algorithm that generates a checksum that is generally used to detect errors in data transmission. You might see the following values when using a hash algorithm:

- CRC-16 produces a 16-bit checksum.

- CRC-32 produces a 32-bit checksum.

- MD5 produces a 128-bit hash.

- SHA-224 produces a 224-bit hash.

> **Important note**
> A checksum is a shorter value as its purpose is to detect transmission errors. Although this value is important, it does not have as rigorous requirements as a hash value, which is used in a cryptographic function to ensure data integrity.

In addition to generating a fixed-size output, the algorithm must always return the same hash value, as discussed next.

Consistently creating the same hash

Deterministic means that the algorithm will produce the same hash every time the algorithm is run on a given block of data. This property is important, as any changes to the output will indicate that there has been some modification to the data.

Even so, it's important to protect the message digest and provide assurance that it was sent from an authorized sender.

For example, imagine the following scenario when sending a document to someone:

- A malicious actor could intercept and make changes to the document.

- The malicious actor could then redo the message digest, and then send the document to the intended recipient.

Even though the original message digest was replaced by the malicious actor, the recipient will have the correct hash value, as the hash value was also replaced.

To protect against this type of attack, the sender should use an HMAC. That way, if a malicious actor were to intercept and change the message digest, the recipient would know that the message digest was invalid because the message digest would not be encrypted.

Another key property is making sure that no two hash algorithms are the same.

Ensuring collision resistance

Collision resistance means that it isn't possible to have two different messages with the same hash value. Every hash algorithm has the potential for a collision. However, it's optimal to have *strong* collision resistance, especially when used in cryptographic applications.

Let's compare weak and strong collision resistance.

Weak collision resistance

With some algorithms, there may be a possibility of having two inputs that will result in the same hash value. For example, the CRC-32 algorithm was used in the **Wired Equivalency Protocol** (**WEP**). The algorithm was found to be prone to attacks, which could result in a malicious actor being able to modify the contents of a message. Algorithms that have weak collision resistance are unsuitable for cryptographic techniques.

Strong collision resistance

On the other hand, new hash algorithms approved by the **National Institute of Standards and Technology** (**NIST**) are found to have strong collision resistance. One such algorithm is Keccak (pronounced "catch-ack"), which was the winner of the SHA-3 competition in 2012. You can read more here: `https://www.nist.gov/news-events/news/2012/10/nist-selects-winner-secure-hash-algorithm-sha-3-competition`.

Now that we understand some of the optimal hash properties, let's investigate some of the algorithms in use today.

Comparing common hash algorithms

Similar to the choices we have when using encryption, there are several hash algorithms. Each one compresses the data a bit differently in order to create a message digest. In this section, we'll review some of the more common hash algorithms in use today and see why some are more secure than others.

First, we'll take a look at an early hash algorithm, the message digest algorithm, and then discuss SHA. Then we'll review some of the versions of SHA that are more acceptable hash algorithms used for cryptographic processes. Finally, we'll briefly discuss some of the permutation-based hash algorithms that are starting to gain traction, as an even more secure cryptographic option.

Let's start with one of the earliest cryptographic hashes, the message digest algorithm.

Using the message digest algorithm

Hashing a block of text produces a message digest. Ronald Rivest designed the aptly named message digest algorithm, which had several versions.

The first functional algorithm was MD4, developed in the early 1990s. MD4 accepted a variable-length input and produced a 128-bit message digest. This was achieved by compressing a 512-bit block of text using three rounds. Early on, MD4 was considered to be insecure as the algorithm was prone to collisions.

The next version of the message digest was MD5. Rivest improved the algorithm, which is similar to MD4. However, MD5 uses an additional round of compression (four rounds), which improved the security. MD5 was used for several years as an accepted algorithm for the following applications:

- File integrity
- **Secure Sockets Layer (SSL)**
- **Internet Protocol Security (IPsec)**
- Storing passwords

Most applications have moved away from using MD5 in cryptographic applications, such as a digital signature, as it has been proven to be vulnerable in that it can be prone to collisions. However, you will see the MD5 algorithm being used in certain applications.

Another significant hash algorithm is SHA. Let's take a look.

Exploring the Secure Hash Algorithm (SHA)

The SHA was developed by NIST in the early 1990s. The SHA family has several members, each designed to be used for an approved U.S. **Federal Information Processing Standard (FIPS)**. However, the SHA algorithms have been adopted worldwide for general cryptographic purposes.

The progression of SHA is as follows:

- **SHA-0** was developed in 1993 and produced a 160-bit message digest. Because of significant weaknesses in the algorithm, it was soon replaced by the next iteration, SHA-1.

- **SHA-1** was an improved version of the algorithm and was published in 1995. SHA-1 also produced a 160-bit message digest; however, the construct was closer in design to the MD5 algorithm. The **National Security Agency (NSA)** designed the algorithm and was an integral part of the Digital Signature Standard.

- **SHA-2** was another improvement in the SHA family. This version has two members, SHA-256 and SHA-512. The two differ in how they process data. SHA256 is designed for operating systems that use 32-bit registers, such as old Windows OSes, and SHA-512 is designed for operating systems that use 64-bit registers.

- **SHA-3** is a permutation-based hash algorithm, also known as Keccak. This version is SHA is the most promising as it provides a robust hash with exceptional performance. The algorithm is unlike classic algorithms in that the technique has a sponge construct.

> **Important note:**
> A sponge construct is a permutation that *absorbs* data and then *squeezes* out data in a variety of sizes, which provides greater flexibility.

Most will agree that SHA-2 and SHA-3 are considered more secure and should be used in cryptographic applications.

Of course, there are other hash algorithms. Let's discuss a few.

Recognizing other hash algorithms

If you do a search for hash algorithms, you will see that there are many others. Some examples are as follows:

- **Whirlpool** is a hash algorithm developed in 2000 by one of the co-creators of the **Advanced Encryption Standard** (**AES**). The algorithm generates a 512-bit message digest and performs functions similar to AES: SubBytes, ShiftColumns, MixRows, and AddRoundKey.

- CRC is a family of lightweight hash algorithms used in a variety of applications, such as error detection during data transmission and file integrity.

Over the years, there have been several hash algorithms used in cryptographic applications. However, some have been deprecated, mainly because they are not able to withstand an attack. In 2004, NIST issued a statement saying that because of the vulnerabilities, the use of MD5 would be phased out of any (U.S.) federal applications. In addition, NIST also felt that it was best to move away from SHA-1 as well, which was phased out of use in 2010.

Nevertheless, as we have seen, there several other secure options. When considering algorithms, NIST will continuously test and suggest algorithms that are considered to be the most secure when creating a message digest. Currently, NIST recommends that SHA-2 and SHA-3 should be used for cryptographic techniques. You can read more here: `https://csrc.nist.gov/projects/cryptographic-algorithm-validation-program/secure-hashing`.

One of the significant uses of a hash algorithm is message authentication. Let's explore this next.

Authenticating a message

When providing message authentication, we have several methods that can provide assurance that the message came from an authorized sender and was not modified during transmission.

In this section, we'll take a look at creating a MAC using symmetric encryption for a single message such as a document. Then we'll take a look at using a MAC while encrypting data.

Let's start with how we can create a MAC.

Creating a MAC

A MAC is a code that authenticates or verifies the sender. To provide message authentication, we can use the following:

- Asymmetric (public key) encryption. We covered this method in *Chapter 5 Dissecting Asymmetric Encryption*, in the *Creating a digital signature* section.

- Symmetric encryption using a shared secret key.

Either method can be used when sending a message across an insecure network. The method used will depend on the application.

Let's outline what happens when creating a MAC using symmetric encryption. In this example, Alice needs to send a message to Bob. Because the message is important, Alice and Bob will use a MAC, as shown in the diagram:

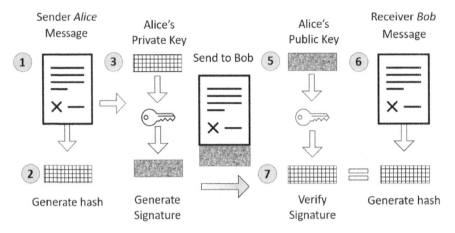

Figure 6.9 – Creating a MAC using conventional encryption

Let's step through the process:

1.   We begin with the message on Alice's (the sender) side.

2.   The algorithm generates a hash of the message.

3.   The hash is encrypted using the shared secret key and the encryption algorithm, which becomes an HMAC.

4.   The message is sent to Bob (the recipient).

5.   The hash is removed and is decrypted using the shared secret key and the decryption algorithm, which assures message authentication.

6.   The algorithm generates a hash of the original message.

7.   The two hash values are compared. If they match, we are assured there has been no violation of integrity.

This method provides assurance that the message wasn't modified by a malicious actor. However, keep in mind that while message authentication is important, it does not provide confidentiality and the data could be exposed.

If the data must be encrypted, there are options for this as well. Let's explore how this is done.

Encrypting and authenticating data

In addition to using a MAC between two individuals, it can also be used during transmission of a large amount of data. The following methods not only provide message authentication, but will encrypt the data as well.

One example is **Cipher Block Chaining - MAC (CBC-MAC)**, which is a technique that provides message authentication when using the CBC mode of operation.

CBC-MAC uses the underlying CBC mode, as discussed in *Chapter 4, Introducing Symmetric Encryption*, in the *Comparing symmetric operation modes* section. As shown in the graphic, we see the CBC mode:

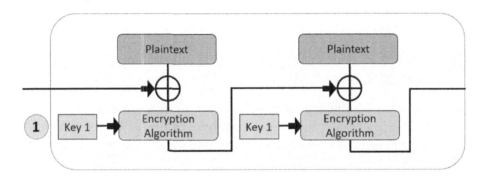

Figure 6.10 – CBC mode

In this case only one key is used to encrypt data. However, when using CBC-MAC, there is also an authentication code, as shown on the lower right-hand of the graphic:

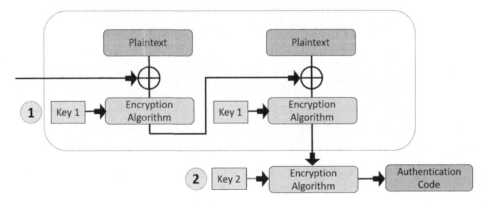

Figure 6.11 – CBC-MAC

CBC-MAC uses the chaining mode and encrypts and authenticates data. However, in this mode there is a distinct difference from just using CBC. Instead of only using a single shared key, the CBC-MAC mode uses two shared secret keys:

1. Key 1 is used to encrypt during the chaining process.

2. Key 2 is used for message authentication.

In this mode, you *must* use two separate keys or you will risk an attack and data exposure. In addition, changing the keys periodically will improve security.

A CBC-MAC is not the only method to provide encryption and message authentication for a large amount of data. Other methods include the following:

-   The **Nested MAC (NMAC)** algorithm

-   The **Cipher-based MAC (CMAC)**

-   The **Parallel MAC (PMAC)** algorithm

Using a MAC is a versatile cryptographic technique that provides sender verification, which is powerful when dealing with unknown entities on the network. Couple a MAC with encryption and you will have confidence that your data will arrive safe and secure.

Summary

In this chapter, we learned how a hash algorithm is a one-way function that takes a variable-length block of text and creates a fixed-length output. The output is referred to as a message digest. A message digest can be used in a variety of applications. We saw how it can ensure file integrity, create a digital signature, or verify a password. In addition, we can use a hash to identify data within a hash table and create a blockchain.

Not all hash algorithms are created equal in that there are several optimal hash properties. We reviewed these properties, including the one-way nature of the algorithm in that the message digest bears no resemblance to the original text. We also saw how a hash needs to consistently create the same hash every time the algorithm is run on a block of data. And we learned that one of the more important properties is collision resistance.

We reviewed several common hash algorithms, namely those in the message digest and SHA families. We know that there are choices in hash algorithms. However, only SHA-2 and SHA-3 are considered robust enough to be used in a cryptographic application. Finally, we reviewed ways to provide message authentication for either a single message or a large block of text.

In the next chapter, you'll learn how various laws and guidelines outline specific rules on how to ensure the protection of our data. We'll cover the **Payment Card Industry Data Security Standard (PCI DSS)** and the **Health Insurance Portability and Accountability Act (HIPAA)**. We'll also review several others so you can better understand how they set guidelines on protecting data. In addition, we'll see how cybercriminals use encryption for nefarious ways, such as to slip into a system undetected and to conceal malware. We'll also see how government and law enforcement agencies seek to decode encrypted data on phones or computers during an investigation.

Questions

Now it's time to check your knowledge. Select the best response, then check the answers in the *Assessment* section at the end of the book:

1. When generating a hash, we create a message _____, which is used to ensure data integrity.

    a. chain

    b. digest

    c. key

    d. collision

2. During the digital signature process, the message digest is then encrypted using the sender's private key, which then becomes a(n) _____.

    a. key

    b. collision

    c. smart card

    d. HMAC

3. Today, there are billions of devices on the **Internet of Things (IoT)**. The data generated by IoT devices is called _____ data.

    a. big

    b. key

    c. Rivest

    d. collision

4. A hash algorithm should be _____; this means that the algorithm will produce the same hash each and every time the algorithm is run on a given block of data.

a. ElGamal

b. round

c. deterministic

d. Galois

5. Ronald _____ designed the aptly named message digest algorithm, which had several versions in the early 1990s.

a. Rivest

b. Enigma

c. ElGamal

d. Rijndael

6. SHA-3 is a permutation-based hash algorithm, also known as _____. This version of SHA is the most promising as it provides a robust hash with exceptional performance.

a. ElGamal

b. Keccak

c. Rijndael

d. Feistel

7. A _____ is a technique that provides message authentication when using a block cipher.

a. round function

b. sponge grip

c. CBC-MAC

d. Rivest

Further reading

Please refer to the following links for more information:

- To learn how a MAC is used to authenticate a message, visit `http://www.crypto-it.net/eng/theory/mac.html`.

- Visit `https://ww1.microchip.com/downloads/en/AppNotes/00730a.pdf` to discover how to calculate a cyclic redundancy check.

- To see how Hadoop is used to harness big data, visit `https://blog.scottlogic.com/2016/01/13/introduction-to-hadoop-and-map-reduce.html`.

- Read about WEP security issues here: `http://www.isaac.cs.berkeley.edu/isaac/wep-faq.html`.

- Learn more about the attacks on MD4 and MD5 here: `https://csrc.nist.gov/News/2004/NIST-Brief-Comments-on-Recent-Cryptanalytic-Attack`.

- We can see an article written by Ronald Rivest on MD4 here: `https://dl.acm.org/doi/10.5555/646755.705223`.

- View this article to learn how a hash table is created: `https://www.tutorialspoint.com/data_structures_algorithms/hash_data_structure.htm`.

- Read up on what the Keccak team is doing here: `https://keccak.team/`.

- For a detailed discussion on message authentication, visit `http://www.crypto-it.net/eng/theory/mac.html`.

Section 3: Applying Cryptography in Today's World

In this section, we'll see the practical aspects of cryptographic techniques. We'll cover the standards that drive the need to encrypt and secure data. You'll learn the importance of the **Public Key Infrastructure (PKI)** in ensuring trust among entities. In addition, you'll see how we can securely transmit data by using either an **Internet Protocol Security (IPsec)** or **Transport Layer Security (TLS) Virtual Private Network (VPN)**. We'll then review how, given the many attacks designed to alter the integrity of our data and systems, there is a need to protect cryptographic techniques. Finally, we'll recognize how advances in technology will require stronger algorithms to encrypt and secure our data.

This section comprises the following chapters:

- *Chapter 7, Adhering to Standards*
- *Chapter 8, Using a Public Key Infrastructure*
- *Chapter 9, Exploring IPsec and TLS*
- *Chapter 10, Protecting Cryptographic Techniques*

7
Adhering to Standards

Along with all the connected systems, devices, and interactivity, we also see an expansion of the amount of data. With this expansion comes the need to ensure the confidentiality, integrity, and availability of the data. In this chapter, we'll provide an overview of how security standards and laws exist to provide guidelines and best practices to prevent data loss. We'll review some of the guidelines provided by the **Federal Information Processing Standards (FIPS)** along with the **Payment Card Industry Data Security Standard (PCI DSS)**.

In addition, we'll see that there are strict legislative requirements such as the **Health Insurance Portability and Accountability Act (HIPAA)** and the **General Data Protection Regulation (GDPR)**. We'll also see how state guidelines such as the **California Consumer Privacy Act (CCPA)** necessitate due diligence and due care in securing data. Although most of us use encryption to protect our digital data, we'll discover how malicious actors have found novel ways to use encryption, which include concealing malware and ransomware. Finally, we'll cover how various laws are designed to provide a back-door policy so that government and law enforcement agencies have a method to decrypt digital data.

In this chapter, we're going to cover the following main topics:

- Understanding FIPS and PCI DSS

- Staying compliant

- Leveraging encryption

Understanding FIPS and PCI DSS

Every day more and more information flows across our networks and the internet, over multiple platforms. Along with the volume of data exchanged, there is an increased concern about the security of the data.

In general, you might think that businesses and organizations will do what is necessary to secure our digital data, however, that is not always the case. Over the past decade, billions of high-profile data breaches have occurred, which makes it more evident that organizations need firm guidelines on the way they protect our data.

In this section, we'll take a look at how security laws and standards provide specific guidelines on how to prevent data from being compromised in some way.

Let's start with an overview of FIPS.

Outlining FIPS

When interacting online, users enter information when submitting applications, posting on social media, and purchasing goods and services. Businesses and organizations have a responsibility to secure data and protect information. When dealing with choices as to how to secure the data, there are many resources that provide good practice guidelines. One resource is FIPS. FIPS standards were developed at the **National Institute of Standards and Technology (NIST)**. Please refer to the following link for more information on NIST: https://www.nist.gov/. NIST is a US government agency that provides information on a range of topics that include the following:

- Advanced communications

- Quantum science

- Forensic science

- Cybersecurity

NIST helps industries in providing research in science, standards, and technology. FIPS are in line with federal government requirements for handling digital data. One of the US government standards is the **Federal Information Security Management Act (FISMA)**.

Although the guidelines are designed to provide a road map for US government agencies, the general public is welcome to reference the standards for their own information. Using the government standards can provide confidence in properly handling digital data.

The standards outline several areas that deal with encryption such as hashing, encryption algorithms, and standards when creating a digital signature. Let's review these concepts, starting with the Secure Hash Standard.

Secure Hash Standard (SHS)

A hash algorithm is a one-way function that takes a given input (of any size) and produces a fixed-length output. The output size will depend on the algorithm and is commonly referred to as a *message digest* or *fingerprint*. Message digests are used to ensure integrity as any change to the document will change the value.

> **Important note**
>
> A message digest is called a fingerprint because, similar to a fingerprint used in biometrics, the message digest uniquely identifies the message.

Hash algorithms are used in a number of different cryptographic techniques, which include storing a password, verifying the integrity of a file you have downloaded, and blockchain technology.

The SHS outlines the various hash algorithms that are considered to be secure when creating a message digest, and are all in the **Secure Hash Algorithm (SHA)** family. The following hash algorithms are included: *SHA-224, SHA-256, SHA-384, SHA-512, SHA-512/224*, and *SHA-512/256*.

> **Important note**
>
> SHA-1 was one of the early versions of the Secure Hash Algorithm. However, it has been deprecated and is no longer recommended by NIST. For more information, visit `https://csrc.nist.gov/projects/hash-functions/nist-policy-on-hash-functions`.

Next, let's take a look at the Advanced Encryption Standard.

Advanced Encryption Standard (AES)

AES is the US government standard for encrypting and decrypting data. Also known as the *Rijndael algorithm*, AES is a symmetric encryption algorithm, in that it uses a *single shared key* (or *secret key*). AES is a block cipher that can encrypt a block size of 128 bits using key lengths of either 128, 192, or 256 bits.

Another standard that is defined by FIPS is the Digital Signature Standard, as outlined next.

Digital Signature Standard

A digital signature provides message authentication for digital documents. To provide a consistent secure method of creating a digital signature, the **Digital Signature Standard (DSS)** became a FIPS government standard in 1994. The standard defines the parameters for proper construction of a digital signature, which include the following:

- The **Digital Signature Algorithm** (**DSA**), which specifies how to generate a key pair

- An approved hash algorithm (such as SHA-512) used to create the message digest

The signature can be used on objects such as documents and digital transactions to provide assurance that the object originated from the claimed signatory. In addition, it provides assurance that there were no modifications of the data during transmission.

FIPS has other standards listed, designed to provide guidelines and best practices to prevent data loss. Another set of guidelines is PCI DSS. Let's take a look at this in the next section.

Outlining PCI DSS

One standard that outlines exact requirements for safely handling data is PCI DSS. This specifies the controls that must be in place to securely handle credit card data. Controls include methods to minimize vulnerabilities, employ strong access control, along with consistently testing and monitoring the infrastructure.

Unlike laws that are created by a government, PCI DSS is a standard that was created by a group of major credit card companies in 2006. Some of the card companies involved in this process included *MasterCard*, *Visa*, *American Express*, and *Discover*. At that time, the card companies felt it was paramount to define guidelines that listed best practice methods to have more control over cardholder data.

PCI DSS documentation is found at `https://www.pcisecuritystandards.org/pci_security/`. Within the documentation, you will find a list of four main tenets and guidelines, which include the following:

- Reasons why the standards exist

- A definition of the standards

- Methods to secure the data

- Metrics to determine the security level of cardholder data

Let's review each of these, starting with outlining why the standards exist.

Learning why the standards exist

In the early 2000s, more and more businesses were going online. Along with this transition, businesses, organizations, and governments saw the value in accepting credit card data while shopping. However, along with this growth, there came the need to secure digital transactions. PCI DSS was developed to help outline standards that minimize exposure and fraud for anyone that deals with credit cards.

Malicious actors attempt to obtain credit card information, such as account number and other elements necessary to impersonate the cardholder. In addition to digital transactions, credit card theft can occur in many places, which include customer databases, a **Point of Sale** (**POS**) terminal at a restaurant, or even records in a filing cabinet. The standards exist as a way of dealing with the threats to the security of cardholder data, whether online or at a brick-and-mortar store.

Next, let's take a look at what the standards outline.

Defining PCI DSS standards

The attack vectors and threats to credit card data can be vast. To address this, PCI DSS standards provide granular details on methods to secure data. Within the framework, there are six categories that describe what is required. The categories list a specific goal, and then define the requirement. To summarize, an organization must do the following in order to protect cardholder data:

- Create and maintain a secure infrastructure by using dedicated appliances and software that monitor and prevent attacks.

- Employ good practice strategies, such as changing passwords from the vendor default, and training users not to open suspicious emails.

- Protect cardholder data using encryption, whether at rest or in motion across a network. In addition, employ proper management of the encryption keys.

- Continuously monitor for vulnerabilities and utilize appropriate anti-malware protection that is continuously updated.

- Provide strong access control methods by using the principle of least privilege, and routinely monitor and test networks.

In addition, the organization must create and maintain appropriate information security policies that define rules of proper behavior.

The goals cover all good practice requirements that any organization should follow.

Summarizing methods to secure the data

PCI DSS compliance relies on a continuous process of assess, remediate, and report. By using the prescribed controls, this ongoing process provides the greatest level of security. The elements in this process are further defined as follows:

- **Assess** means taking inventory of all assets and locations where cardholder data can be found, such as a POS terminal, websites, and even paper records. Once that is complete, the next step is to identify all vulnerabilities.

- **Remediate** means taking steps to mitigate or repair the vulnerabilities and enact secure business processes. In addition, merchants should avoid storing any cardholder data if possible.

- **Reports** of the assessment process and any mitigation details are created and then disseminated to the bank and proper card company.

A company must be vigilant and make efforts to secure the data. However, a company's best effort may not be enough. The only way to tell if they have achieved the goal of being PCI DSS compliant is by completing an assessment and then reporting the results. Let's see what's involved, next.

Measuring the security level

PCI DSS is not a law, therefore there is no government oversight. However, it's imperative that anyone that deals with cardholder data must comply with the guidelines. If a merchant fails to comply and is in violation of the requirements, they can face a substantial fine, and even lose the ability to handle credit card transactions.

The security level will define whether the merchant must complete a self-assessment or have an external auditor assess that the merchant is compliant. In addition, the level defines whether they must complete a **Report on Compliance (RoC)**. Therefore, the first step is to identify how many transactions are done on a yearly basis. Once the transaction value is determined, the merchant is then ranked.

The levels are as follows:

- **Level 4**: Is a small merchant with under 20,000 transactions a year
- **Level 3**: Is a merchant with 20,000 to 1 million transactions a year
- **Level 2**: Is a merchant with 1 to 6 million transactions a year
- **Level 1**: Is a large merchant with over 6 million transactions a year

The activity required, for each level required to prove compliance with the guidelines, is as follows:

- **Level 1**: Must have an external auditor perform the assessment by an approved **Qualified Security Assessor (QSA)**
- **Levels 2-4**: Can either have an external auditor or submit a self-test that proves they are taking active steps to secure the infrastructure
- **Levels 1 or 2**: Must complete an RoC

> **Important note**
> PCI DSS offers a self-validation assessment tool that steps through every aspect of the standard. You can find the link in the *Further reading* section.

As PCI DSS standards can be complex and overwhelming, vendors provide platforms that help ensure compliance, as outlined in this document by Cisco: `https://www.cisco.com/c/en/us/solutions/enterprise-networks/pci-compliance/index.html`.

Over the years, there have been numerous data breaches that have resulted in millions of records being compromised, along with exposure of **Personally Identifiable Information (PII)**. As a result, various laws are in place that define controls that must be in place to ensure the security and privacy of personal data. Two such laws are GDPR and HIPAA, as outlined next.

Staying compliant

The number of individuals connecting to the internet is expanding at a rate of approximately 10 percent every year. Along with this expansion, we are also seeing more personal data being collected, curated, and stored for a variety of uses. Data is collected in many different ways, which include the following:

- Vehicles and navigation apps

- Online shopping and banking

- Health care and wearables that monitor fitness level

- Utility companies such as water, electricity, and gas

- Devices on the Internet of Things

Called big data, this digital ocean has the potential to do remarkable things that can improve our lives. Many companies see the value in using this data, for marketing campaigns, managing risk, improving the supply chain, and other applications. The data is fed into apps such as intelligent decision support systems, that optimize artificial intelligence to provide predictive responses.

Because of all of the data being exchanged, governments have enacted laws designed to protect our privacy. In the US and the **European Union** (**EU**), there are several laws that deal with the protection of consumer data. In this section, we'll take a look at the key components of HIPAA, GDPR, and the CCPA, which outline specific rules on how to ensure the protection of personal data.

Let's start with a law that safeguards the privacy and security of patient information in the US.

Ensuring the privacy of patient data

In the 1990s, health care facilities began implementing computer technology to store patient data. At that time, someone could walk up to a unit clerk in the hospital and inquire about the status of their neighbor. There were no privacy laws, and the fact that medical records were being computerized made it easy for someone to retrieve the information and share it with anyone.

Concurrently, computerization and networks began to expand, and along with it came concerns about data privacy. This prompted legislative action to protect patient data. In 1996, the US government enacted a federal law to protect the privacy and security of patient data. Called the **Health Insurance Portability and Accountability Act** (**HIPAA**), the law provides rigorous requirements for anyone dealing with patient information.

Computerized electronic patient records are referred to as **electronic protected health information (e-PHI)**. With HIPAA, the e-PHI of any patient must be protected from exposure, or the organization can face a hefty fine.

While many refer to HIPAA as the *privacy rule*, there are actually two components: the *privacy* rule and the *security* rule. The *privacy* rule outlines specifications for assuring the privacy of patient data. The *security* rule defines methods to put into operation the privacy rule requirements. This is achieved by specifying the technical and non-technical methods to monitor and prevent attacks and protect the infrastructure.

HIPAA outlines the following guidelines that organizations must follow:

- Any and all e-PHI that is generated, obtained, stored, or exchanged must be kept confidential.

- Any and all e-PHI must be kept in an unaltered form, and available to anyone that has the right and privilege to access the data.

- Proactively monitor for threats, mitigate vulnerabilities, and maintain a secure infrastructure by using methods that monitor and prevent attacks.

- Prevent exposure of e-PHI by using technical and non-technical methods that include physical, technical, and administrative safeguards.

- Educate all personnel in the workforce and ensure that everyone involved in handling patient data, from onsite employees to outsourced contract workers, respects the confidentiality of patient data.

It's in everyone's interest for an organization to exercise due diligence and due care in ensuring the privacy of patient data. Violations of privacy affect both the medical provider and the patient. A medical provider can receive a fine from $100 to $50,000 per violation and will most likely suffer from a loss of goodwill. An affected patient could suffer consequences of identity theft, which could have lasting implications.

In addition to HIPAA, there are other laws that govern the treatment of consumer data. Let's investigate GDPR, next.

Giving consumers control of their data

In 2018, the EU enacted the General Data Protection Regulation, which outlines specific requirements on how consumer data is protected. The law affects *anyone* who does business with residents of the EU and the UK. This comprehensive law focuses on the privacy of consumer data, and more importantly, gives consumers the ability to control how their data is handled.

Some of the components of this law include the following:

- **Requiring consent**: If a company wants to gather information on your searching and buying patterns, it must obtain your permission to acquire and use your information.

- **Sharing information**: In addition to obtaining permission to *acquire* your information, a company must obtain your permission to *share* your information. For example, if a company obtains your email address, and they want to share it with a sister company, they must first obtain your permission.

- **Rescinding consent**: Just as the consumer can give consent for a company to use their information, they can opt out at any time. Known as the *right to be forgotten* rule, this puts control back in the hands of the consumer.

- **Global reach**: The GDPR affects anyone who does business with residents of the EU and Britain. The statute directly relates to e-commerce, as websites do not have a physical boundary. If you do business with anyone in the EU or the UK, this rule will prevail.

- **Restricted data collection**: Organizations should collect only the minimal amount of data that is needed to interact with the site.

- **Violation reporting**: If the company's consumer database is compromised, they must report the breach within 72 hours.

While you are surfing the internet, checking news feeds, and shopping online, websites can collect data about you. This is done using cookies while interacting with a website and is one example of how GDPR impacts the consumer, as discussed next.

Harvesting data

Hypertext Transport Protocol (**HTTP**) is a stateless protocol that doesn't retain any information about a transaction. In order to retain information about your visit, and make a website more interactive and personalized, websites can use cookies, which are small text files. Within the cookies, there can be information on your browsing habits, items you put in your shopping cart, and possibly PII.

As a result, when you go to a website, you will see a banner with a statement on the use of cookies as shown here:

We use cookies on our site so that we can provide an optimal experience for you, as we provide custom content and advertising. To learn more, visit our Privacy Policy.

Because cookies can harvest information and be shared with other parties, this falls under the GDPR guidelines. Specifically, a company can use consumer data, as long as they have obtained permission.

If a company violates consumer privacy, they can be fined. Knowing this, most companies strive to adhere to the regulations as outlined by the GDPR.

Many countries implement laws that deal with the privacy of an individual. In addition, in the US, there are several states that have enacted their own privacy policy. One state is California, as we'll see next.

Enforcing protection in California

California has long been a leader in technology and laws that deal with the privacy of consumer information. The California Consumer Privacy Act was enacted in 2018 and outlines specific guidelines on how to appropriately handle consumer data.

Companies can store basic data, such as names, email and home addresses, phone numbers, and birthdays. However, depending on the application, the consumer data can also include credit card information, social security numbers, and even **Global Positioning Satellite (GPS)** coordinates.

In addition to companies sharing and selling consumer data, there is also the threat of a data breach, which can expose the PII of millions of consumers. The CCPA is similar to GDPR; the law lists specific regulations that affect anyone who does business with California residents.

The requirements of the CCPA include the following:

- Transparency in what data is being stored
- The right for consumers to easily opt out and be wiped from the company's database
- The ability to request that their data not be shared or sold to third parties
- If there is a data breach, the company can be fined $100 to $750 per consumer

Many have grown weary of the vast amounts of exposed data, so laws such as the CCPA are a welcome relief. While these are a few examples of laws that protect consumer data, experts predict that more laws will require more measures aiming to protect the network, data, and consumer privacy.

As outlined, there are many ways we can use encryption. Most of the time it is used to protect our data from unauthorized access. However, malicious actors have found ways to leverage encryption for their own purposes. Let's investigate these concepts in the next section.

Leveraging encrypted data

The cryptographic algorithms and protocols developed over the years were primarily focused on securing data. However, like a two-edged sword, encryption can be used for malicious reasons.

In this section, we'll review how we use cryptographic techniques to help secure and protect our data. We'll then examine ways cybercriminals use encryption, such as concealing malware or holding our data hostage. In addition, we'll discuss how government and law enforcement agencies seek to decode encrypted data on phones or computers during an investigation.

Let's start with reviewing ways that cryptographic techniques help secure our data.

Securing our data

Today, there are many things that threaten the security of our data. As a result, we remain vigilant in protecting our networks and data from attacks or unauthorized access. On any network, there are several goals or services we strive to provide, such as confidentiality, integrity, authentication, and non-repudiation.

Some of the security services we use help ensure the data is not modified, lost, or accessed in an unauthorized manner. Cryptography helps protect our passwords, wireless transmissions, email, and e-commerce transactions.

However, malicious actors are finding ways to use encryption that can threaten the security and integrity of our systems. Next, let's take a look at how criminals use encryption to slip malware onto a network undetected.

Concealing malware

Imagine, when monitoring your network using Wireshark, a packet analysis tool, you might see traffic as shown in the following screenshot:

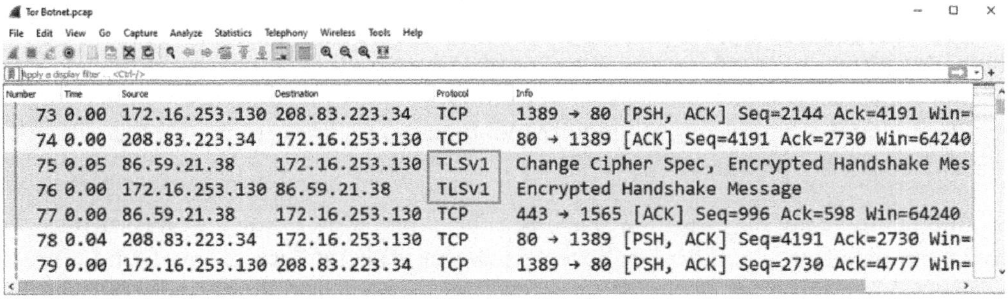

Figure 7.1 – TOR activity on a network

The traffic appears innocent, as we can see **Transmission Control Protocol** (**TCP**) traffic along with **Transport Layer Security** (**TLS**) traffic. TLS is used when communicating with a website using HTTPS. However, upon further investigation, we see that a malicious actor is using **The Onion Router** (**TOR**) to communicate. TOR is an internet-based system that encrypts traffic.

Because TOR uses encryption, this masks the fact that, in this case, the malicious actor is delivering malware designed to infect systems with cryptojacking malware. *Cryptojacking* is malicious cryptomining, which uses the victim's resources to mine cryptocurrency.

When using an encrypted communication channel (such as TOR) the malicious actor can do the following:

- Deliver malware undetected and infect a system.
- Set up communication with a **command and control** (**C&C**) server.
- Mine the victim's machine and send results back to the server.

All of this is done in plain sight, as the activity is undetected, therefore difficult for antimalware protection to analyze.

> **Important note**
> We'll learn more about TLS in *Chapter 9, Exploring IPsec and TLS*.

Using encryption to conceal malware continues to be a threat. In 2021, over 25% of malware communicates using TLS, and the numbers continue to rise.

In addition to using encryption to deliver malware, malicious actors use encryption to lock out users and hold a system hostage.

Holding files ransom

Ransomware is a form of malware that holds data hostage until a payment or ransom is paid. Unlike a worm, which can move throughout a system without a transport agent, ransomware gets onto a system by getting a victim to perform some action. The action can be clicking on a link, opening a file, or going to a website.

Encrypting ransomware works in the following manner:

1. The malicious actor will use a carefully written phishing or spear-phishing email to get past the spam filters.

2. The email gets into a user's inbox with the hope that the user will open the email and perform some action, such as opening an infected Adobe PDF or Microsoft Excel file.

3. Once the ransomware is released, it can complete any number of different actions, such as spawning child processes, encrypting files, deleting shadow copies, blocking access to your system, and stopping applications from running.

4. The ransomware immediately attempts to communicate with the C&C server to receive further instructions.

5. Soon afterward, the C&C server will display a message demanding a ransom that if the victim does not pay, the malicious actor will destroy the decryption key. In addition, they can unleash malware designed to delete all the files on the system.

The victim may pay the fine, however, there is no guarantee that the malicious actor will release the files. Therefore, it's best to take steps to avoid a ransomware attack.

While not acting in a malicious manner, another issue related to encryption is forcing individuals to expose their private information. Let's discuss this next.

Exposing private information

Over the years, it has become more important to protect our digital transmissions from prying eyes. A couple of examples where data transmissions could be intercepted include the following:

- **Phone conversations**: Almost all voice traffic is digitized and transmitted over the internet using **Voice over Internet Protocol** (**VoIP**). This makes it very easy for anyone to eavesdrop on unencrypted traffic to hear a phone conversation.

- **Email**: Email is critical to business and is also used by a large majority of those who are online. Similar to VoIP, anyone can read unencrypted email messages.

In the US, cryptography is legal. Therefore, to secure our digital data, we use encryption. However, a government official or law enforcement agency might want to view the contents of your email or listen to your phone call. As a result, there might be a law or statute that allows the government to decrypt your data. Let's explore this concept, next.

Gaining access to encrypted data

If law enforcement or government officials need to gain access to encrypted data, there may be a legitimate reason. For example, they might request access to internet traffic so they can monitor for unlawful activity, such as child exploitation or human trafficking. However, for a government law official to listen in on conversations, they would need to obtain a warrant, so they could monitor for possible illegal activity.

Over the years, various bills were submitted to Congress to allow backdoor access to someone's encrypted conversations or email during an investigation. In addition, there have been several accounts of government or law enforcement agencies attempting to force a user to provide a key to decrypt data. Some of the bills and government activity aimed at being able to view encrypted data include the following:

- In 1993, the US government proposed the use of a *Clipper Chip*, which enabled law enforcement to decode encrypted voice traffic.

- In 1994, US Congress passed the **Communications Assistance for Law Enforcement Act (CALEA)**, which provided the ability to wiretap phone systems.

- In 2018, FBI Director *James Comey* tried to force Apple's hand to decrypt data held on an iPhone.

We use encryption for a number of different reasons. One is that we want to ensure the confidentiality of our data and keep private data private. However, if someone has a way to provide back door access to view our data, it's not possible to provide any security at all.

Summary

In this chapter, we covered how various laws and standards provide specific guidelines and best practices to prevent data from being compromised in some way. We reviewed key components of FIPS and PCI DSS, outlined why the standards exist, and how they are used to ensure the protection of data. We then reviewed how, in the US and the EU, there are several laws that deal with the protection of consumer data.

We discussed how key components of HIPAA, GDPR, and the CCPA outline specific rules on how to ensure the protection of personal data. Finally, we covered different ways we can leverage the use of encryption. We know that we use encryption to secure our data and prevent unauthorized access. However, we learned how malicious actors use encryption in a malicious way, to conceal malware in a stream of encrypted data, or encrypt and lock files until a ransom is paid.

In the next chapter, we'll outline some common attacks on encrypted data along with some advanced attacks that can threaten the effectiveness of cryptographic techniques. We'll then learn how the public key infrastructure can also be a target and suffer from attacks such as a TLS strip, along with other exploits. Finally, we'll review the fact that our current encryption algorithms have protected our data for decades. However, we'll see how quantum computing may be able to decrypt data with ease and render current encryption algorithms obsolete.

Questions

Now it's time to check your knowledge. Select the best response, then check your answers with those found in the *Assessment* section at the end of the book:

1. The _____ outlines the various hash algorithms that are considered to be secure to used when creating a message digest and all in the **Secure Hash Algorithm (SHA)** family.

    a. AES

    b. SHS

    c. PCI DSS

    d. SSL

2. _____ specifies the controls that must be in place to securely handle credit card data.

    a. AES

    b. SHS

    c. PCI DSS

    d. SSL

3. _____ is a law that outlines rigorous requirements for anyone dealing with patient information.

    a. e-PHI

    b. PCI DSS

    c. GDPR

    d. HIPAA

4. In 2018, the EU enacted the _____, which outlines specific requirements on how consumer data is protected.

    a. e-PHI

    b. PCI DSS

    c. GDPR

    d. HIPAA

5. _____ is a form of malware that holds data hostage until a payment or ransom is paid.

    a. Ransomware

    b. Clipper Chip

    c. PGP

    d. e-PHI

6. Almost all voice traffic is digitized and transmitted over the internet using _____, which makes it very easy for anyone to eavesdrop on unencrypted traffic to hear phone conversations.

    a. Clipper Chip

    b. VoIP

    c. PGP

    d. SHS

7. In 1994, the US Congress passed the _____, which provided the ability to wiretap phone systems.

    a. CALEA

    b. SHS

    c. GDPR

    d. HIPAA

Further reading

Please refer to the following links for more information:

- For a list of current standards for the FIPS, visit `https://www.nist.gov/itl/current-fips`.

- Visit `https://csrc.nist.gov/publications/detail/fips/186/5/draft` to review the **Digital Signature Standard (DSS)**.

- For a complete list of all the parameters that are assessed during a PCI DSS compliance check, visit `https://www.pcisecuritystandards.org/documents/PCI_DSS_v3-2-1.pdf?agreement=true&time=1604781332907`.

- To view the *PCI DSS Self-Assessment Questionnaire D*, visit `https://www.pcisecuritystandards.org/documents/PCI_DSS_v3-1_SAQ_D_ServiceProvider_rev1-1.pdf`.

- Find out more on HIPAA at `https://www.hhs.gov/hipaa/index.html`.

- Go to `https://thenextweb.com/contributors/2019/01/30/digital-trends-2019-every-single-stat-you-need-to-know-about-the-internet/` to find a variety of statistics about the internet.

- Visit `https://www.malwarebytes.com/cryptojacking/` to learn more about cryptojacking.

- To understand the implication of sharing data under the GDPR, visit `https://21ilab.com/blog/gdpr-consent-in-company-groups/`.

- To read how much malware is communicating using TLS, visit `https://news.sophos.com/en-us/2020/02/18/nearly-a-quarter-of-malware-now-communicates-using-tls/`.

- To read more on ways the US government wants to build backdoor access into encrypted devices, read `https://cdt.org/insights/issue-brief-a-backdoor-to-encryption-for-government-surveillance/`.

- To see a list of countries that impose restrictive laws that govern the use of cryptographic techniques, visit `https://www.comparitech.com/blog/vpn-privacy/encryption-laws/`.

8
Using a Public Key Infrastructure

Malicious actors constantly launch assaults on a network, such as malware, spoofing, and **Denial of Service (DoS)** attacks. As a result, during a data transaction on a network, it's important to have the confidence that you are communicating with an authorized entity. A **public key infrastructure (PKI)** enables the secure exchange of data between two parties.

In this chapter, we'll learn how a PKI is the cornerstone for most digital transactions that require encryption. We'll outline how a PKI provides the trust required when exchanging data, and how components (such as algorithms) and a **certificate authority (CA)** work together. Next, we'll see how a PKI manages, securely stores, and distributes session keys, along with outlining the difference between a trusted root certificate and a self-signed certificate. So that you understand the many moving parts of a transaction, we'll examine the heart of a PKI: the elements within an X.509 certificate. Finally, we'll see the different methods used to provide validation, along with some of the ways in which we use a digital certificate.

In this chapter, we're going to cover the following main topics:

- Describing a PKI framework
- Managing public keys
- Examining a certificate

Describing a PKI framework

If you see a lock by the web address when making a transaction on the internet, as shown in the following screenshot, you can be confident the site is secure:

Figure 8.1 – The Packt Publishing website showing a lock to indicate a secure site

The lock represents trust, which means that when exchanging data with the website, your data is secure. A PKI verifies the identities of both parties so that they can encrypt and securely exchange information.

This trust is possible because of a PKI—a framework used to generate, manage, and distribute digital certificates.

A PKI framework helps to ensure data confidentiality and integrity and is essential for several applications, such as securing email and encrypting data transactions.

In this section, we'll see how a PKI ensures trust and allows us to securely exchange keys during a data transaction, along with some of the different components of a PKI. In addition, we'll discuss where we store certificates and learn what happens when a certificate is no longer valid.

Let's start with how a PKI provides trust between two parties.

Understanding how a PKI assures trust

During data transactions on a network, cryptographic tools, techniques, and protocols ensure the confidentiality and integrity of the data. However, it's critical to provide trust among all participants.

We address the issue of trust on a network in several ways, that includes:

- **The web of trust** is a concept that uses a trusted introducer that assigns a level of confidence for each key. When using the web of trust model, each individual manages their own set of keys.

- **Kerberos** is an authentication protocol used within Microsoft **Active Directory (AD)** that uses a client-server configuration to issue session keys to entities within a domain.

- A **CA** is a PKI component that generates a digital certificate to securely distribute keys between a client and a server during a transaction.

While all three preceding models provide the same functionality, they differ in capacity and scale. Of the three, a CA has the largest scope and continues to scale with ever-evolving network demands.

> **Important note**
>
> PKIs have expanded and evolved over time. However, in the future, there may be challenges in keeping up with demand. One key reason is that many of the billions of devices on the **Internet of Things (IoT)** may require the use of a PKI for secure data transactions.

While meeting the need for trust among communicating parties is essential, one of the main reasons for using a PKI is to securely deliver the keys used during data transmission. Let's explore this, next.

Exchanging the keys

During a secure data transaction, we use keys to encrypt the data. The key chosen will depend on the type of algorithm in use, outlined as follows:

- **Symmetric encryption**: Uses a single shared (or secret) key

- **Asymmetric encryption**: Uses a pair of keys: a public key and a private key

When securely exchanging data across a network, the data is encrypted using symmetric encryption, which uses a single shared key. Prior to the data transaction, each party must obtain the same shared key.

Let's discuss ways to achieve this goal.

Obtaining the same shared key

If you recall from *Chapter 5, Dissecting Asymmetric Encryption*, one approach to obtaining the same shared key is to use **Diffie-Hellman (DH)**, a key agreement protocol. However, the problem with DH being the sole method to do this is with trust, in that the entities are not natively authenticated.

Another way for each party to obtain a copy of the same shared key is by using asymmetric encryption. When using asymmetric encryption, an entity's private key is kept private. In contrast, a public key is shared for everyone to see, as it is public. To share a public key, it can be published on a key server, sent via email, or even posted on a web page.

When obtaining someone's public key for a transaction, we need to be able to trust that the key is from a reputable source, and not an imposter. For example, if we need to use Alice's public key, we need to make sure the key came from Alice, and not someone else pretending they are Alice. As a result, one of the best ways to obtain the same shared key is to use PKI with certificates.

> **Important note**
>
> A newer method to distribute keys is called **quantum key distribution (QKD)**. Because of the ever-increasing need to secure data transactions, industry experts are constantly seeking ways to improve security while keeping up with technology. **Quantum key management (QKM)** uses quantum mechanics to produce a **shared secret (SS)** key. While some companies utilize QKM on a limited basis, the field is still largely experimental.

Next, let's take a look at the components that make up a PKI framework.

Understanding the components

Within a PKI framework, there are many components that make the system work. In this section, we'll cover some of the main elements—such as the algorithms—along with the CA.

Let's start with the different algorithms used during a transaction.

Providing the algorithms

A PKI is based on cryptographic tools, algorithms, and protocols. The algorithms that are required include the following:

- An asymmetric encryption algorithm—such as **Rivest-Shamir-Adleman (RSA)**, the **Digital Signature Algorithm (DSA)**, or **Elliptic Curve Cryptography (ECC)**—that is used to generate a key pair

- A hash algorithm that includes any of the **Secure Hash Algorithm (SHA)** family members, such as SHA-256 and SHA-512

The algorithms that are used must be the same on both the client and server side and are generally agreed upon during the handshake process.

We'll also need a CA. Let's take a look at a few recognized CAs in use today.

Employing a CA

A CA represents a trusted third party in a cryptographic framework—such as a PKI—that both parties trust. Some companies that provide certificate services are listed here:

- **Let's Encrypt** provides a no-cost **domain validation (DV)** certificate. Let's Encrypt, located at `https://letsencrypt.org/`, is open source and is an optimal choice for someone with a small company website, as a certificate can add validity to that company.

- **Comodo** offers a variety of encryption choices, and users can get a free DV certificate on a trial basis. With some options, there is an opportunity to add a Comodo logo to build client trust. Find more information on this here: `https://ssl.comodo.com/`.

- **GoDaddy** has evolved over the years to be one of the largest CA and web hosting platforms worldwide. With its size, it is able to offer a variety of certificates, many of which are reasonably priced. For more information, visit `https://www.godaddy.com/web-security/ssl-certificate`.

Of course, there are other large CAs. When deciding on which CA to partner with, it's best to do your research to select the CA that can provide the best certificate for your company's needs.

One consideration of clients is to have a location to store certificates. Let's discuss this next.

Storing certificates

During the many data transactions that we have on a daily basis, you will most likely gather many certificates. A certificate store is a location where the operating system stores certificates from many different CAs. A macOS operating system will store these certificates in a virtual keychain. On a Windows operating system, you can find your certificates using the **Microsoft Management Console** (**MMC**) snap-in, as shown in the following screenshot:

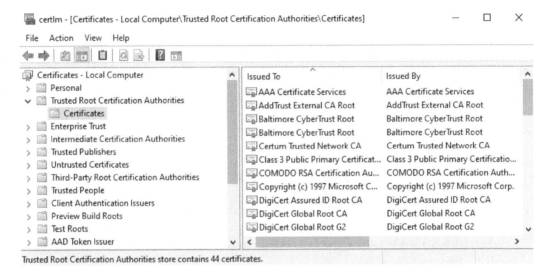

Figure 8.2 – The MMC Certificates snap-in

Once you have opened the snap-in, you can view details for each of the certificates.

We know that certificates are essential for secure data transmissions. However, there are times when a certificate becomes outdated or is no longer trusted. Let's explore what happens when this occurs.

Revoking a certificate

When using a PKI, an important element of the framework is being able to trust all entities. The certificate from the CA is a foundational element of this trust. All web browsers have a list of CAs and information on whether a certificate is valid or has been revoked.

Certificates can be revoked for a number of different reasons, such as the issuing company is no longer in business, the certificate has expired, or the CA's private key was somehow compromised.

If a certificate is found to be untrusted, you will most likely get an error on your browser. For example, I purposely changed the date on my computer to March 2, 2039 and then went to Google. The browser then presented this error:

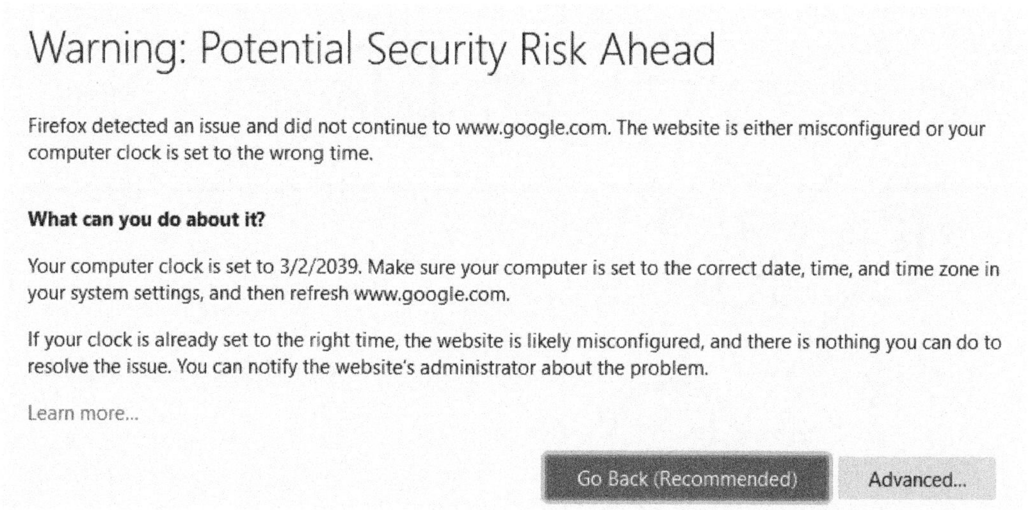

Warning: Potential Security Risk Ahead

Firefox detected an issue and did not continue to www.google.com. The website is either misconfigured or your computer clock is set to the wrong time.

What can you do about it?

Your computer clock is set to 3/2/2039. Make sure your computer is set to the correct date, time, and time zone in your system settings, and then refresh www.google.com.

If your clock is already set to the right time, the website is likely misconfigured, and there is nothing you can do to resolve the issue. You can notify the website's administrator about the problem.

Learn more...

Go Back (Recommended)   Advanced...

Figure 8.3 – Warning from Google

Each certificate contains a serial number, which provides a unique identification. When beginning a transaction, the status of the certificate is checked by using one of the two following methods:

- A **certificate revocation list (CRL)**
- The **Online Certificate Status Protocol (OCSP)**

A CRL is a list of certificates that have in some way been deemed invalid. Although CRLs are effective, most online services have moved to the newer OCSP to check the validity of the certificate.

This process is shown in the following screenshot:

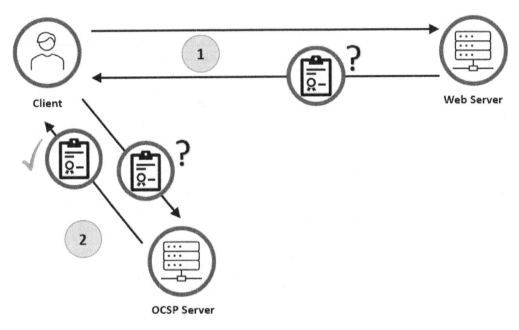

Figure 8.4 – Standard OCSP process

Let's take a look at how this works. When a client goes to a web server to initiate a transaction, the following process occurs:

1. The web server sends the client the certificate.

2. The client then goes to the OCSP server to check the validity of the certificate.

While this is a valid process, another way to achieve this is by using certificate stapling. Let's see why this improves efficiency.

Stapling a certificate

In the standard approach to determining the validity of a certificate, the burden rests on the client, who must check the certificate's validity with the OCSP server.

Stapling a certificate reverses this burden, so the *web server* must validate the certificate, as shown in the following screenshot:

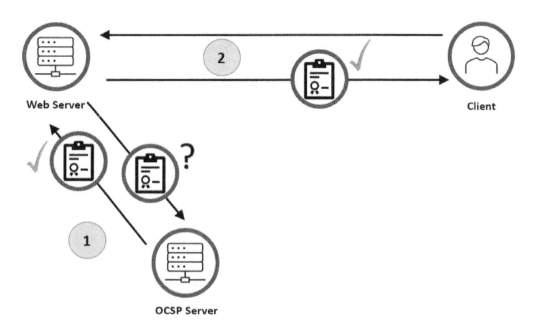

Figure 8.5 – OCSP process using stapling

With certificate stapling, when a client begins a web server transaction, the following process occurs:

1. The web server goes to the OCSP server to check the validity of the certificate.

2. The web server then sends the validated certificate to the client.

As shown, there are several elements within a PKI framework. Another vital consideration is effectively creating a certificate and managing the keys. Let's see what's involved in this process, next.

Managing public keys

A PKI is responsible for securely delivering verified public keys, which provides assurance or trust that you are communicating securely with a verified entity. A PKI achieves this goal by using a digitally signed certificate.

In this section, we'll discuss what's involved when creating a certificate. We'll see how malicious actors can intercept and spoof certificates, along with how pinning can help prevent this from happening. Finally, we'll compare trusted root certificates with self-signed certificates and see the steps to take to create a self-signed certificate on a Windows machine.

First, let's step through creating a certificate.

Creating a certificate

When a company wants to create a digital certificate that links a public key with their organization, they will go through a formal process. The first step is to create a **certificate signing request (CSR)** that is sent to the CA.

Let's see what's involved in a CSR.

Requesting a signed certificate

The Kiddikatz pet store needs a digital certificate for their company website. Kiddikatz must send their public key, along with a CSR that provides information on the company. This generally includes the following information:

- **Common Name (CN)**: This represents the name of the web server. When submitting, it must include the domain and hostname (if applicable). Have a look at the following examples:

  - Kiddikatz is applying for a certificate specifically for the `Pets` subdomain. In that case, the submitted common name should be `pets.kiddikatz.com`.

  - Kiddikatz is applying for a certificate for just Kiddikatz.com. In that case, the submitted common name should be `kiddikatz.com`.

  The information must be spelled and presented correctly. If it is not correct, the client will receive an error when trying to reach the server.

- **Organization (O)**: This represents the legal name of the company and any additional identifiers—for example, Kiddikatz **Limited Liability Corporation (LLC)**.

- **Organization Unit (OU)**: This represents the department that manages the certificate—for example, the OU could be the Sales department or the **Information Technology (IT)** division.

- **Locality (L)**: This represents the city where the company is located.

- **State or Province Name (ST)**: This represents the state or province where the company is located.

- **Country (C)**: This represents the country where the company is located.

- **Email Address (email)**: This represents the email address of the certificate manager. It's best to keep this generic and not use a real employee name—for example, `webmaster@kiddikatz.com`.

- **Signature Algorithm**: This represents the algorithms used when generating the certificate. For example, the algorithm selected might be listed as follows:

  - **The asymmetric encryption algorithm**: RSA encryption

  - **The hash algorithm**: SHA-2

> **Important note**
>
> When using RSA encryption, you might be presented with an option to select a key length. A common key length is 2,048 bits; however, some CAs will offer larger key lengths.

- **Public key**: This represents the public key that is to be included in the certificate.

Once the CSR is complete, it can be sent to the CA for signing. Let's take a look what's involved, next.

Submitting the CSR

Once the CSR is complete, the request can be sent to the CA, as shown in the following screenshot:

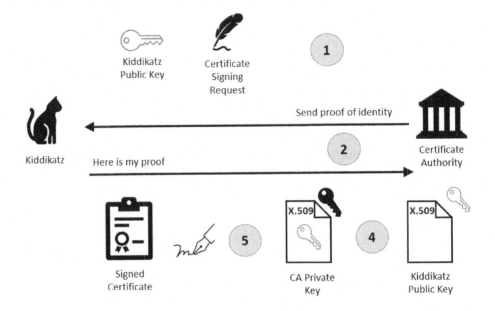

Figure 8.6 – Creating a digital certificate

In this example, the Kiddikatz pet store needs a digital certificate for their organization. Let's step through the process shown in the preceding screenshot, as follows:

1. The CSR and the Kiddikatz public key are sent to the CA.

2. The CA will request that Kiddikatz send proof of their identity.

3. Once Kiddikatz's identity is verified, the CA will add the Kiddikatz public key to the X.509 certificate.

4. The CA creates a digital signature using the CA's private key.

5. The signed certificate is then sent to Kiddikatz.

Now that the CA has created the certificate, Kiddikatz can use this to provide a secure transaction whenever someone visits their site.

A certificate can be trusted root, intermediary, or self-signed. Let's compare the differences.

Trusting the root

When looking at the details of a certificate, you will commonly see a certificate path, as shown in the following screenshot:

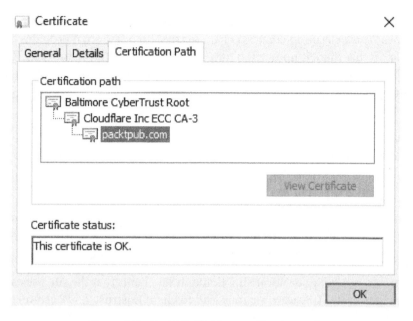

Figure 8.7 – Packt Publishing certification path

The different levels exist because when dealing with CAs, there are often several levels involved.

Understanding the path

When a certificate is issued to a company, the certificate is at the end of the path. This is because the certificate was most likely obtained by an intermediate CA.

If you look at the Packt Publishing **Certification path**, you'll see the following levels:

- The first level represents the root CA. In this case, the root CA is Baltimore CyberTrust Root.

- The second level represents the intermediate CA, which is Cloudflare Inc ECC CA-3.

- The third level represents the certificate for Packt Publishing, packtpub.com.

Let's outline how this works.

At the root level, there is a fairly small number of high-level CAs. The root CAs include companies such as Comodo Cybersecurity, GeoTrust, GoDaddy, and Verisign. Because this small number of CAs deal with entities worldwide, it's necessary to have intermediate CAs so that they can issue certificates as well.

The root CAs delegate trust to the intermediate CAs, which in turn provide certificates for companies. This delegation creates a chain of trust. In addition, it provides a layer of protection, in that there is no need to have direct contact with the root CA. This protection is critical, as if the root CA were to be compromised this could have serious downstream implications, as the security breach would affect all lower-level CAs as well. As a result, the root CA many times is simply taken offline.

When discussing certificates, another term you might hear is self-signed certificate. Let's discuss what this means.

Defining a self-signed certificate

If a certificate is said to be self-signed, this means that someone has simply vouched for themselves. Using a self-signed certificate is not advised. If a self-signed certificate is used on a website, there may be multiple issues, including the following ones:

- The browser might issue a warning that notifies clients that the site uses a self-signed certificate. This warning may lead to client mistrust, and customers might be hesitant in interacting with the site, which could lead to a potential loss of revenue. This is especially true in sites that deal with e-commerce or banking transactions.

- Because a self-signed certificate lacks authentication, an attacker can more easily spoof the certificate with a bogus certificate.

- A self-signed certificate isn't managed in the same way as one issued by a CA, therefore if the certificate were to be compromised, this would cause difficulties in revoking it.

While a self-signed certificate isn't practical for use in real life, it can be used for testing purposes. In addition, a self-signed certificate can be used on a small private network, but in general is not advised.

> **Important note**
> While a self-signed certificate isn't advised, the one exception is the root CA, which signs its own certificate.

A CA is a trusted third party in a PKI. As a result, it is essential to protect CAs from theft or modification. Let's see how we can achieve this goal.

Protecting a CA

The root CA is the most critical CA in a PKI, and root certificates generally have rigorous security controls. However, it's also good practice to protect your CA servers as well, and—more specifically—the CA's private key.

To protect the CA servers, here are a few best-practice guidelines to follow:

- Implement strong physical security for all servers and server rooms.
- Perform regular security audits and make sure your server operating system is up to date on patches and the latest antimalware protection.
- Regularly back up your certificate databases.
- Use strong password protection on the server and, if possible, use **multi-factor authentication (MFA)**.

We know that for a production network or a website, a certificate obtained for a CA is advised. However, a self-signed certificate can be used for your own personal use, such as a signing code that you created. Let's see how this works.

Creating a self-signed certificate

Within the Microsoft Office suite of products, there are many tools users can employ to streamline their work. One such tool is a macro, which is a small block of code that can be run to achieve a specific task. For example, if you want to create a macro that adds a signature at the end of a document, you can create one in Word. You would need to go to **View** and then **Record Macro...**, as shown in the following screenshot:

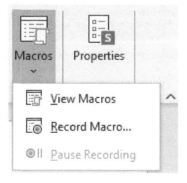

Figure 8.8 – Recording a macro

To create a self-signed certificate in Windows, navigate to `Program Files | Microsoft Office | root | Office16`, as shown in the following screenshot:

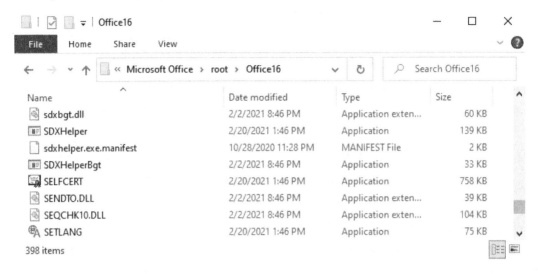

Figure 8.9 – Selecting the SELFCERT option

Once in the folder, select the **SELFCERT** option, which will open a dialog box. Once there, enter the name of the certificate, as shown in the following screenshot:

Figure 8.10 – Creating a digital certificate

When you select **OK**, a dialog box will be displayed, notifying you that the **SelfCert** was a success, as shown here:

Figure 8.11 – Dialog box showing the SelfCert creation was a success

Once you create a certificate, you can then view it by going to **Tools** and then **Internet Options**, which will bring up the **Internet Properties** dialog box. Select the **Content** tab, as shown in the following screenshot:

Figure 8.12 – Internet Properties dialog box

Once there, you can select **Certificates**, which will open the **Certificates** options. Select the **Personal** tab and you will see your newly created certificate, as illustrated in the following screenshot:

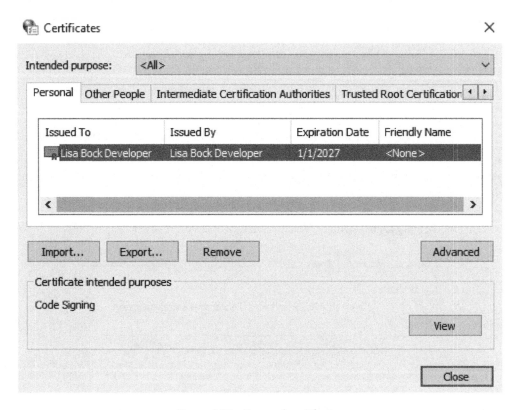

Figure 8.13 – Personal certificates

To read more information on how you can acquire a digital certificate to create a digital signature, visit https://support.microsoft.com/en-us/office/obtain-a-digital-certificate-and-create-a-digital-signature-e3d9d813-3305-4164-a820-2e063d86e512.

As we can see, the trust we have in a certificate is critical in ensuring secure digital transactions. However, during a transaction, a malicious actor can intercept a certificate and present a spoofed certificate to the client. Let's see how this is possible, and then discuss steps to take to avoid this type of attack.

Spoofing the process

When setting up a **Transport Layer Security (TLS)** session, a client could be the victim of a **Man-in-The-Middle (MiTM)** attack. In a MiTM attack, a malicious actor sits in the middle of the communication stream and intercepts the genuine certificate. The malicious actor then passes a bogus certificate to the client, as shown in the following screenshot:

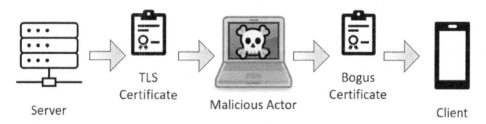

Figure 8.14 – MiTM attack

Instead of receiving the expected certificate from the web server, the client will receive a bogus certificate. This is possible because an application on the client side won't always check the certificate, especially on a mobile device.

In some cases, there might be a notification from the operating system that the certificate is not recognized. This may be followed by a prompt that asks if the client would like to accept the certificate. If the user accepts the certificate, a spoofed certificate will be placed in the certificate store and will be accepted as valid, and the transaction will continue in a normal fashion. The malicious actor will then be able to see details of the transaction.

Now that we know this is possible, let's see how pinning a certificate can prevent this from happening.

Pinning a certificate

There are some applications that require a client to always use the same server (such as a gaming server). If this is the case, a developer can pin or hardcode a certificate right into the application. This will prevent a user from accepting another (bogus) certificate, as pinning makes it clear that the certificate will not change. If any changes are made to the certificate, the client should report this as this may be a security issue.

As we have learned, a certificate is a set of descriptive data that provides a way to ensure that you can *trust* the public key you use when exchanging data. In the next section, let's see what's included in a digital certificate.

Examining a certificate

The foundation of a PKI is the contents of an X.509 certificate. X.509 is the format a CA uses to provide assurance that a public key belongs to an entity contained within a certificate.

In this section, we'll take a high-level look at a certificate and then see what's involved in the X.509 standard. Then, we'll see the different ways a certificate can be validated and compare the many ways one can be used today.

Let's start with taking a high-level look at a certificate.

Viewing a certificate

When you are on a secure site, you will see a lock. When selected, the dialog box will drop down and assure you that the site is secure, as shown here using Mozilla:

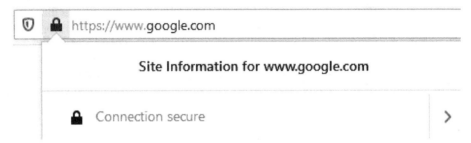

Figure 8.15 – Google secure connection

While in the Mozilla browser, if you select the arrow to the right of the **Connection secure** notification, you can expand the information. You can then select more information (found at the bottom of the dropdown), which will bring up a larger dialog box called **Page Info**.

Once on the **Page Info** dialog box, if you select the **Security** icon (shown as a lock) you will see that there is a great deal of information on the website, including the following: **Website Identity** and **Privacy & History**, along with **Technical Details**, as shown in the following screenshot:

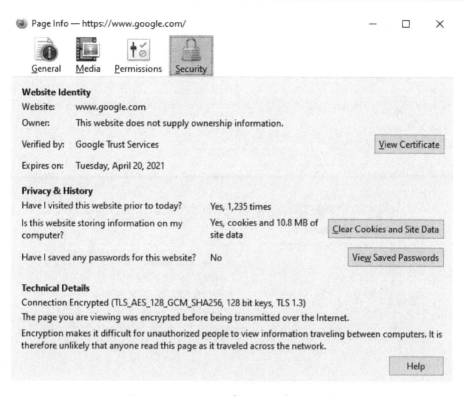

Figure 8.16 – Page information for Google

To view the certificate, select **View Certificate**, which will open a new page where you can view all details of the certificate, as shown here using the Mozilla browser:

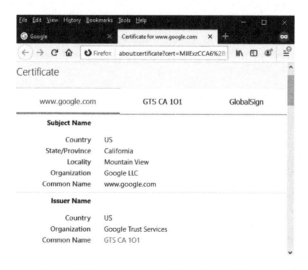

Figure 8.17 – Beginning of Google's certificate

Other browsers will display the certificate details differently—for example, the following screenshot shows the certificate details for Chrome:

Figure 8.18 – Google's certificate in Chrome

As shown, there are a variety of ways to view details of a certificate. However, the one constant across most certificates is the X.509 standard, as outlined next.

Recognizing the X.509 standard

The X.509 standard provides a format for creating a certificate and includes the following elements:

- **Version** represents the X.509 version that was used to create the certificate. In *Figure 8.18*, we see **V3**, which is version 3.

- **Serial number** represents the unique identifier of the certificate.

- **Signature algorithm** lists the algorithm used to sign the certificate. In *Figure 8.18*, we see the **sha256RSA** algorithm listed.

- **Signature hash algorithm** lists the hash algorithm used when signing the certificate. In *Figure 8.18*, we see the **sha256** algorithm listed.

- **Issuer** is the name of the entity (generally a CA) that issued the certificate.

- **Validity** is the time period during which a certificate is valid. In *Figure 8.18*, we see the **Valid from** field populated with **Tuesday, January 26, 2021** and the **Valid to** field populated with **Tuesday, April 20, 2021**.

- **Subject** shows the name of the entity the CA issued the certificate to. This should match the name of the site you are visiting. In Google's certificate, the subject is ***google.com**.

- **Subject public key** is the public key of the entity.

- **Extensions** are optional; however, these are often included in a certificate.

While most certificates appear to be similar in nature, not all are validated in the same manner. Next, let's see the different types of certificate validation.

Validating a certificate

When vetting a certificate, there are several different types of validation, each having different requirements that must be provided prior to obtaining the certificate. Validation types include the following:

- **DV** is a simple method that validates only the domain name, which would be appropriate for a basic site—for example, a club or organization.

- **Organization validation** (**OV**) has more rigorous requirements and is used to validate the legal identity of a business or organization, which helps provide reassurance to clients.

- A **wildcard** is used when you need a certificate to secure subdomains for a single domain. For example, when using a wildcard for `Google.com`, you would enter the following: `*google.com`. You would then see the subdomains listed under **Subject Alternative Name** in the certificate details, as shown in the following screenshot:

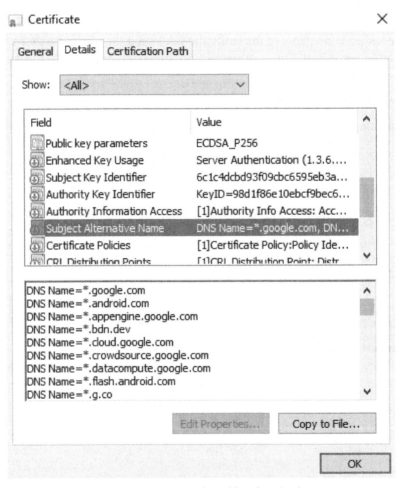

Figure 8.19 – Using the wildcard method

- A **Multi-Domain Certificate** (**MDC**) is used when an organization has several domains within the organization. For example, the Kiddikatz empire could include the following domains: `kiddikatz.com`, `wolfdog.com`, or `orangetigerkittens.com`.

- A **Unified Communications Certificate** (**UCC**) is similar to an MDC, as it allows several domains to be secure under one certificate. The idea of this stemmed from Microsoft servers involved in unified communication (such as Lync, Microsoft Exchange, and Microsoft Teams) that required a certificate for each server. A UCC solves this issue as the servers can be bundled under one certificate.

When choosing the type of certificate to obtain, a DV is the simplest type. In fact, you can obtain a DV certificate for free with minimal validation at `letsencrypt.org`. However, for an e-commerce site, you would most likely obtain an OV as this provides additional reassurance for a client that a site is not spoofed.

> **Important note**
> **Extended validation** (**EV**) was a rigorous method of providing validation, as a business or organization had to present fully vetted information prior to obtaining this type of certificate. When used, the address bar in the browser would turn green. However, you will most likely not see this type of validation, as EV has been deprecated. You can read more on this here: `https://www.computerworld.com/article/3431667/chrome-firefox-to-expunge-extended-validation-cert-signals.html`.

When using certificates there are different types, depending on how the certificate is used. Let's investigate this, next.

Using certificates

In addition to securing a website, certificates can be used in other ways. The different ways in which certificates can be used include the following:

- A **Secure Sockets Layer** (**SSL**)/TLS **virtual private network** (**VPN**) is one of the most recognized uses for a digital certificate, as this enables a client and server to securely exchange data. A secure site will start with **HyperText Transfer Protocol Secure** (**HTTPS**) and show a small lock icon.

- **Securing email** can be achieved by using one of several standards that provide methods to encrypt email and add a digital signature. Standards include the following: **Pretty Good Privacy** (**PGP**), **Secure/Multipurpose Internet Mail Extensions** (**S/MIME**), and **Privacy-Enhanced Mail** (**PEM**).

- Transporting data using an **Internet Protocol Security** (**IPsec**) VPN. For example, an IPsec VPN can be configured between two firewalls, which will enable secure communication between the two endpoints.

- **Secure Electronic Transaction (SET)** uses certificates while providing the secure transmission of electronically transferred credit card information between card holders, merchants, and banks.

- **Code-signing certificates** are used by software publishers to ensure the validity of their software. When distributing code or updates through third-party sites, this kind of certificate provides reassurance that the software hasn't been altered in any way.

As we can see, there are many elements and types of certificates in use today. It's important to know the differences between them so that you can spot a forgery or other irregularities that could compromise your security.

Summary

In this chapter, we saw how a PKI provides trust while communicating on a network and allows us to securely exchange keys during a data transaction. We saw that a PKI is not a single protocol but a framework comprised of several different components, which include the algorithms, keys, and CAs. In addition, we covered where we store certificates on our own systems and learned what happens when a certificate is no longer valid.

We then took a look at the process of obtaining a digital certificate from a CA. We also discussed ways a malicious actor can intercept and spoof a certificate, and then outlined how pinning a certificate can help prevent spoofing. Finally, we defined trusted root and self-signed certificates and saw the steps to take to create a code-signing certificate on a Windows machine. We then covered what's involved in the X.509 standard, which defines the format of public key certificates. Finally, we saw the different ways a certificate can be validated and compared the many ways in which a certificate can be used today.

In the next chapter, we'll compare two popular VPNs: IPsec and TLS. We'll outline the elements of a VPN, and then explain the concept of an IPsec VPN. Finally, we'll learn about the components of a TLS communication stream.

Questions

Now, it's time to check your knowledge. Select the best response to the following questions and then check your answers, found in the *Assessment* section at the end of the book:

1. X.509 certificates are stored on the operating system. A macOS operating system will store the certificates in a virtual _____.

   a. MMC snap-in

   b. OCSP

   c. keychain

   d. CRL

2. _____ is an authentication protocol used within Microsoft AD that uses a client-server configuration to issue session keys to entities within a domain.

   a. Kerberos

   b. OCSP

   c. Web of trust

   d. MMC snap-in

3. In the standard approach to determining the validity of a certificate, the burden rests on the client, who must check the certificate's validity with the OCSP server. _____ the certificate reverses this burden so that the *web server* must validate the certificate.

   a. Pinning

   b. Stapling

   c. Revoking

   d. Curling

4. The Kiddikatz pet store needs a digital certificate for their company website. Kiddikatz must send their public key along with a _____ that provides information on the company.

   a. PIN

   b. staple

   c. MMC

   d. CSR

5. In the case of certificate _____, a developer hardcodes the certificate right into the application.

    a. pinning

    b. stapling

    c. revoking

    d. curling

6. When submitting a CSR, you'll need to select an encryption algorithm. If you select RSA, you might be presented with an option to select a key length. A common key length for RSA is _____ bits; however, some CAs offer larger key lengths.

    a. 256

    b. 56

    c. 1280

    d. 2048

7. The _____ standard provides a format for creating a certificate and includes elements such as the version, serial number, and subject public key.

    a. X.2048

    b. X.509

    c. Validity

    d. CSR

8. A(n) _____ validation certificate has rigorous requirements used to authenticate the legal identity of a business or organization, which helps provide reassurance to the client.

    a. domain

    b. CSR

    c. organization

    d. stapled

Further reading

Please refer to the following links for more information:

- For an overview of a PKI, visit `https://www.altaro.com/hyper-v/public-key-infrastructure/`.

- To learn more about certificate management and the X.509 chain of trust, visit `https://realtimelogic.com/articles/Certificate-Management-for-Embedded-Systems`.

- For a list of the top five certificate authorities, visit `https://premium.wpmudev.org/blog/ssl-certificate-authorities-reviewed/`.

- To read a comprehensive overview of the many elements of a PKI, visit `https://www.appviewx.com/education-center/pki/`.

- To view a step-by-step guide on how to create and apply a self-signed certificate, visit `https://www.groovypost.com/howto/create-self-signed-digital-certificate-microsoft-office-2016/`.

- To read what's involved in a certificate code-signing request, go to `https://www.thesslstore.com/knowledgebase/ssl-generate/cetificate-signing-request-overview/`.

- Learn how a company can be its own CA by visiting `https://realtimelogic.com/articles/How-to-act-as-a-Certificate-Authority-the-Easy-Way`.

- To compare the different types of certificates, visit `https://www.liquidweb.com/blog/ssl-certificates/`.

- For tips on guarding your CAs, visit `https://www.itprotoday.com/security/guarding-your-certificate-authorities`.

9
Exploring IPsec and TLS

When you begin a data transaction on a network these days, you want to make sure that you can access a resource in a secure manner. One way to accomplish this is by using a **virtual private network** (**VPN**). A VPN is a method used between two endpoints that provides data confidentiality as it crosses through an insecure network. The concept of a VPN has been around for several decades. However, in recent years, this technology has become more popular because with today's changing landscape, a large percentage of the world's population is online. That, coupled with the fact that more and more people are seeking ways to secure their data while in transit, makes using a VPN an optimal solution.

In this chapter, you'll apply all of your knowledge of cryptographic tools, techniques, and protocols as we examine the concepts of a VPN. We'll begin by outlining several types of VPNs in use today, such as **Secure Shell** (**SSH**) and browser-based VPNs for consumers. We'll then explain the concept of an **Internet Protocol Security** (**IPsec**) VPN, compare the two headers, and discover the best choice in selecting an operating mode. In addition, we'll learn how the **Internet Key Exchange** (**IKE**) process provides key management in IPsec. Finally, we'll learn about the components of a **Transport Layer Security** (**TLS**) communication stream and examine the handshake and Record protocols within the TLS framework.

In this chapter, we're going to cover the following main topics:

- Using a VPN

- Outlining an IPsec VPN

- Understanding TLS

Using a VPN

Today, we need to access resources in many ways—from homes, businesses, in airports, or while on vacation. Because of the many threats to our data in a complex world, many businesses and individuals use a VPN to securely transmit data.

> **Important note**
>
> The term *VPN* stems from the idea that the technology secures data that originates in a *private* protected network that must travel across an insecure *public* network.

The concept of a VPN started over three decades ago in the 1990s, when a Microsoft engineer developed the **Point-to-Point Tunneling Protocol** (**PPTP**), which was a precursor to today's VPNs. This functionality was included in Windows operating systems, and businesses soon began using the technology. After setting up a secure tunnel, clients were able to access network resources in the same way they would if they were sitting in the private network, but remotely using cryptographic tunneling protocols.

Time has passed, and today's VPN technology has improved and become adaptable for all types of internet users, including desktop, laptop, and mobile operating systems.

There are many reasons to have a VPN nowadays, as it protects your communication and identity while traversing the internet. A VPN provides the following services:

- **Confidentiality**: Data is encrypted to protect against eavesdropping.

- **Integrity**: Detects any message modification.

- **Authentication**: Ensures only authorized entities are communicating with one another.

In this section, we'll take a look at the choices we have when selecting a VPN, which includes OpenVPN, SSH, and browser-based VPNs for consumers. We'll also take a look at the steps to take to set up a VPN on a Windows machine.

Let's start with OpenVPN.

Securing traffic using OpenVPN

A VPN creates a virtual tunnel by encapsulating data when traveling over an insecure network. There are many choices when selecting a VPN. Some examples include the following:

- **PPTP** was the first VPN and can work with almost any operating system; however, it is not secure and should be avoided.

- **Layer 2 Tunneling Protocol (L2TP)** can work with almost any operating system. L2TP is faster and more secure than PPTP; however, there may be issues when dealing with firewalls.

- **Secure Socket Tunneling Protocol (SSTP)** is an optimal secure solution that is able to deal with firewalls; however, it is only available with a Microsoft operating system.

Another option for consumers is OpenVPN, a freely available open source VPN, found at https://openvpn.net/. OpenVPN has many benefits, which include a high level of security along with the ability to transmit data, using either the **Transmission Control Protocol (TCP)** or the **User Datagram Protocol (UDP)**. OpenVPN can be used on all operating systems, including Windows, Linux, and macOS, along with mobile devices. In addition, it uses TLS, so it is able to traverse through firewalls.

Although OpenVPN is free for consumers, you will need a VPN server. There are many of these available today, including **Private Internet Access (PIA)**, NordVPN, CyberGhost, and others. These services charge a monthly fee, so you'll want to do your research in order to choose an appropriate platform.

In addition to OpenVPN, consumers also have the option to use a browser-based VPN to encrypt traffic while on the internet. Let's talk about this concept next.

Choosing a browser-based VPN

In some cases, you might simply want or need a browser-based VPN to ensure privacy while online. This type of VPN requires minimal setup and can be in the form of an extension or a standalone browser.

One option you can use to encrypt online communications is HTTPS Everywhere, found at `https://www.eff.org/https-everywhere`. This extension can be added to several browsers, such as Chrome, Opera, and/or Firefox. Once you download and install HTTPS Everywhere, you can launch it and begin to browse securely. To modify the settings, simply select the **S** in the right-hand corner of your browser to display a drop-down dialog box, as shown in the following screenshot:

Figure 9.1 – The HTTPS Everywhere extension

To use the extension, turn on HTTPS Everywhere and begin browsing. Keep in mind that not all websites support HTTPS Everywhere, which can therefore leave your data exposed.

Next, let's see what's involved when using an SSH VPN.

Using an SSH VPN

SSH is a technology that allows administrators to securely access remote hosts. The term *shell* means that once you have connected, you will interface with the host using the **command-line interface (CLI)**.

While there are other types of VPNs available, developers and administrators can use an SSH VPN for many different tasks, including the following:

- Accessing cloud databases
- Moving and manipulating files and folders
- Updating software and applying patches
- Managing infrastructure devices such as routers and switches
- Other configuration duties

Accessing SSH in Linux can be done by launching a session within a terminal as SSH is built into the Linux operating system. However, when using the Windows operating system, you'll need to use a third-party app to begin your session as there is no built-in utility. One popular SSH application is PuTTY. Let's see how we can use PuTTY to conduct remote administration.

Using PuTTY to access a remote server

PuTTY is a free SSH client to use on a Windows system, to access a single other host via Telnet and **remote login (rlogin)**. To obtain a copy of PuTTY, go to `https://www.putty.org/`, and from there you can select and download the appropriate version for your system.

After installation, launch PuTTY, and this will bring up a window as shown in the following screenshot:

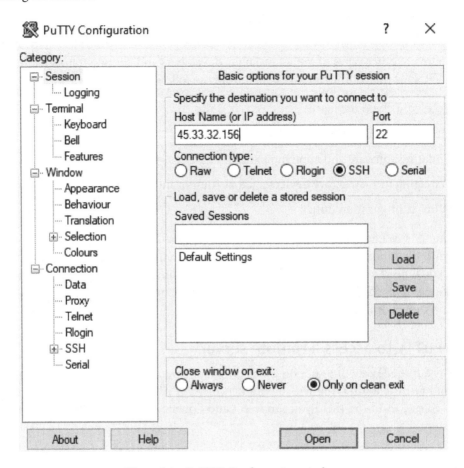

Figure 9.2 – PuTTY Configuration window

Once there, you would enter information in the **Host Name (or IP address)** field. The **Port** field is defaulted at port 22, which is the standard port for SSH. After selecting **Open**, the client and server will complete the following steps:

1. The client initiates contact with the server.

2. The server sends the server's public key to the client, and negotiates the session parameters.

3. The client then completes a login process to begin interfacing with the server.

> **Important note**
>
> Once you begin the setup process, PuTTY will check to see whether the server's key is in your registry. If it is not found, PuTTY will flash a security alert and warn you that the server's public key you are about to accept might be spoofed. This is a precaution as it is meant to protect you from a **man-in-the-middle (MiTM)** attack. Therefore, before accepting the key, you should be absolutely sure that the key belongs to the connecting server.

PuTTY will open a command-line window, where you will see a login prompt to authenticate to the server, as shown in the following screenshot:

Figure 9.3 – PuTTY login

When using SSH, authentication is an essential part of data transaction between hosts. Let's discuss this process next.

Ensuring authentication between hosts

Whenever a client attempts to connect to a host using SSH, there are a couple of methods that the client can use to provide authentication. They can use a username and password, which is generally provided by the administrator, or use **single sign-on (SSO)** with SSH keys.

When using SSH keys, the client will generate a public/private key pair, and then submit their public key to the remote server. When the client requests access, the server will look for the client's public key. Once found, the client will then authenticate to the server using their private key.

If using SSH keys, the client will need a key pair. Let's see how this is achieved.

Generating a key pair

When using SSH, you can generate a key pair in a couple of ways. One way is to use OpenSSH, which can be found here: `https://www.openssh.com/`. However, if you are using PuTTY, you can use the PuTTYgen key generator. Once you launch PuTTYgen, select **Generate** and the app will generate your key pair, as shown in the following screenshot:

Figure 9.4 – Using PuTTYgen to generate a public/private key pair

PuTTYgen has the following field values to enter a comment and a passphrase:

- **Key comment** should include an appropriate name for how the key might be used. For example, I entered `Edge_Router`.

- **Key passphrase** is used to protect the private key. For example, I entered `orangetigerkittens`. You will then be asked to confirm the passphrase.

Using the SSH key option instead of a password to authenticate to a server is a convenient, secure method to interact with a host.

When using an SSH VPN, it's important to protect the SSH keys as they are essentially a password to gain access to the system. If the keys are compromised, an attacker can move through the system and attempt to gain root access.

If you are using the Windows operating system, you can set up a VPN with a few simple steps. Let's take a look.

Using a VPN on a Windows machine

Nowadays, many employers offer flexible work schedules, many of which include the ability to work from home. In some cases, an employee may need to access corporate resources. If that is the case, a VPN will protect data while in transit.

To set up a VPN on a Windows 10 machine, type VPN settings in the search bar, which will bring up this dialog box:

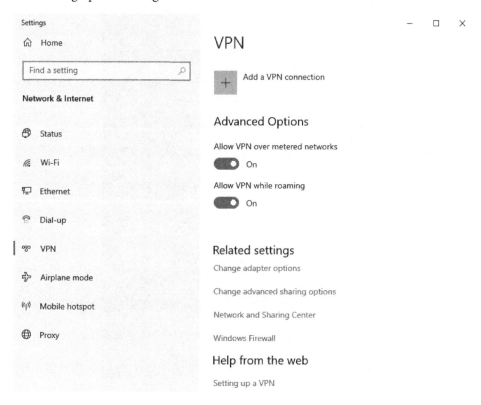

Figure 9.5 – VPN settings in Windows

Prior to launching the wizard, you will need to have contact with the network administrator at the company where you want to connect, to provide information specific to the VPN connection. This information will include the following:

- Server's IP address

- Type of VPN—such as PPTP, L2TP, or SSTP

- Type of sign-in—such as username and password, smart card, **one-time password (OTP)**, or certificate

In addition, they will have to modify settings that will recognize your username and password when you log in to the server.

After you have the information, select **Add a VPN connection**, which will launch the wizard, as follows:

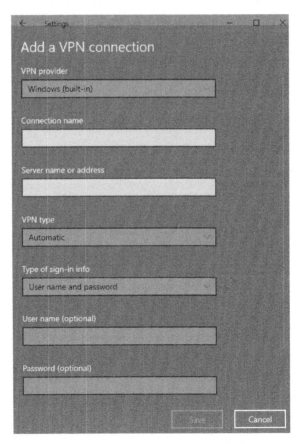

Figure 9.6 – Add a VPN connection wizard

Grasping the IPsec framework

IPsec is not a single protocol, but a framework of protocols and processes that work together to secure data. IPsec can encrypt and authenticate both IPv4 and IPv6 data by using additional headers. IPsec is implemented at Layer 3 of the **Open Systems Interconnection (OSI)** model. As a result, it can protect more applications and layers than TLS, which works at Layer 4 of the OSI model.

Many feel that an IPsec VPN is more secure than TLS, as there are more parameters involved when setting up a connection. In addition, unlike simply using the browser as in TLS, an IPsec VPN requires the use of third-party client software to implement IPsec.

Within the IPsec framework, we see the following elements—the **Encapsulating Security Payload (ESP)** protocol and encryption algorithms, the **Authentication Header (AH)** protocol and authentication algorithms, along with key management, as shown in the following diagram:

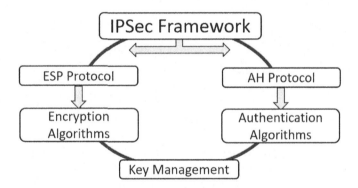

Figure 9.8 – The IPsec framework

When using IPsec, you have a choice as to how your data is protected. The security protocols available include the following:

- The AH protocol authenticates data while assuring data integrity, using a hash algorithm such as **Secure Hash Algorithm (SHA)**.
- The ESP protocol provides confidentiality by encrypting and—optionally—authenticating data using **Advanced Encryption Standard (AES)** as the encryption algorithm.

Key management can be manual in a small environment, or if in an enterprise network, you can use IKE. IPsec also involves a secure key exchange using the DH key exchange protocol.

When using IPsec, there are a couple of common fields for either the AH or the ESP protocols that include the **security association (SA)** and the sequence number. Let's see what's involved in a SA.

Creating a SA

Once the parameters of an IPsec VPN have been configured, a SA is formed between the two hosts. The SA will include parameters such as the security protocols, algorithms, and keys required for the services requested. When using an IPsec VPN between two devices, both sides must share the same SA.

For example, when looking at the IPsec configuration settings on a router, you might see the following inbound SA settings shown here:

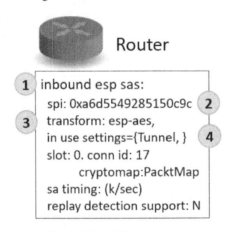

Figure 9.9 – A SA on a router

Within the SA, we see a few descriptive parameters, outlined as follows:

1. `inbound esp sas`: This is the inbound ESP SA.
2. `spi: 0xa6d5549285150c9c`: This represents the **Security Parameter Index (SPI)**, which differentiates the traffic streams that use different encryption rules and algorithms.
3. `transform: esp-aes`: This indicates that this SA will use the ESP protocol and encrypt the data using AES.
4. `in use settings={Tunnel, }`: This indicates that this SA is using tunnel mode.

Each host exchanges its SA parameters with the other host as part of the negotiation process.

Another common field value is the sequence number.

Using the sequence number

Within the ESP and AH headers, there is a sequence number that is a counter of the packet sequence. For example, if you were to view the ESP header in Wireshark, you might see the following field values:

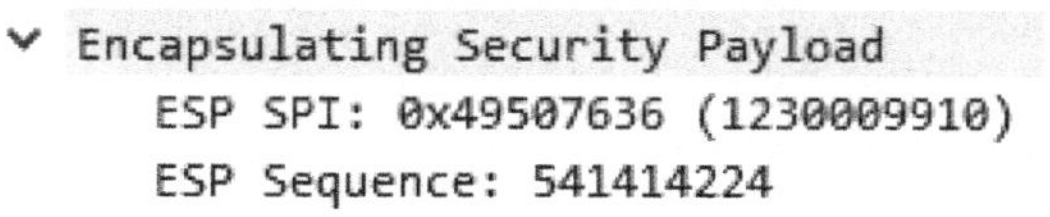

```
✓ Encapsulating Security Payload
      ESP SPI: 0x49507636 (1230009910)
      ESP Sequence: 541414224
```

Figure 9.10 – ESP header in Wireshark

The ESP Sequence number is shown as 541414224, which will increment during the course of the data transaction. The sequence number is used to protect against a replay attack, where a malicious party obtains a packet and then duplicates or replays the packet into the data stream.

A sequence number is always present in either the ESP or AH header; however, it is only used when the SA mandates that the connection is to provide authentication. If authentication is used, the receiving host will check the sequence numbers and reject any packets with a duplicate sequence number as part of the anti-replay protection. In addition, if the sequence number is exhausted, the session must begin a new SA, which reinitializes the counter to 0.

> **Important note**
> The field value for the sequence number is 32 bits; however, many vendors support an extended 64-bit sequence number.

Another key element in IPsec is either the ESP or the AH protocol. Let's see what's involved when deciding which protocol to use.

Selecting the protocols

When beginning an IPsec session, the SA will define the attributes necessary for either the AH or ESP protocols. While there are many choices in terms of algorithms nowadays, the **National Institute of Standards and Technology (NIST) Special Publication (SP)** *800-77 Revision 1* provides guidance on the protocols that should be used to provide authentication, integrity, and confidentiality.

To provide authentication and integrity integrity, use **Hash-based Message Authentication Code (HMAC)** with symmetric encryption will include the following, based on the use of **Secure Hash Algorithm (SHA)**:

- HMAC-SHA256
- HMAC-SHA384
- HMAC-SHA512

To provide data confidentiality, ESP should use AES with a key size of 128, 192, or 256 bits in one of the following modes:

- **Galois/Counter Mode (GCM)**
- **Counter Mode (CTR)**
- **Cipher block chaining (CBC)**
- Counter with **cipher block chaining message (CCM)** authentication code

Keep in mind that over time the protocols may change, so it's best to research your options and use the most secure protocols available.

Now that we know the components of the IPsec framework, let's take a look at the AH and ESP protocols, starting with the AH protocol.

Dissecting the AH protocol

When using IPsec, there are times when only authentication is needed—for example, when two servers need to authenticate with one another on a LAN. The AH protocol provides the following services:

- Assures data integrity
- Provides host authentication
- Protects against replay attacks

The AH protocol has a few key fields, as shown in the following figure:

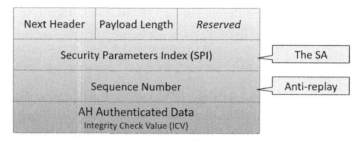

Figure 9.11 – The AH protocol field values

The AH protocol will authenticate all immutable field values in the IP header, along with any protocols in Layers 4-7 of the OSI model. The AH protocol can be used alone or with the ESP protocol in either transport or tunnel operating modes.

Next, let's take a look at an example of the AH protocol in Wireshark.

Using Wireshark to visualize the AH protocol

To see an example of the AH protocol, we'll view an example in Wireshark. If you would like to follow along, go to CloudShark.org where you can obtain the packet capture: `https://www.cloudshark.org/captures/dcbaa6ab009b`.

Once there, you can download and open the capture in Wireshark or continue to use CloudShark. Select `Frame 1` and expand the AH, as shown here:

```
> Frame 1: 194 bytes on wire (1552 bits), 194 bytes captured
> Ethernet II, Src: c2:00:57:75:00:00 (c2:00:57:75:00:00), D
> Internet Protocol Version 4, Src: 10.0.0.1, Dst: 10.0.0.2
˅ Authentication Header
    Next header: Encap Security Payload (50)
    Length: 4 (24 bytes)
    Reserved: 0000
    AH SPI: 0x8179b705
    AH Sequence: 1
    AH ICV: 27cfc0a5e43d69b3728ec5b0
> Encapsulating Security Payload
```

Figure 9.12 – AH in Wireshark

The field values are outlined as follows:

- `Next header` will indicate the protocol that is following the IPsec AH. In `Frame 1`, the next header is the ESP protocol.

- `Length` is how many bytes are in the AH. In `Frame 1`, the length is `24` bytes.

- Reserved is not used and must be set to 0000, as shown in Frame 1.

- AH SPI is the SA used to differentiate the various traffic streams using specific encryption algorithms and policies.

- AH Sequence is a counter of the packet sequence. In Frame 1, the sequence number is 1.

- AH ICV is the **integrity check value (ICV)**, which authenticates the source and verifies the integrity of the payload.

Keep in mind that the AH protocol does not ensure data confidentiality. If data needs protecting with encryption, a network administrator should use the ESP protocol.

> **Important note**
>
> According to NIST, use of the AH should be avoided. Instead, it is recommended that the ESP protocol be used with authentication as it provides confidentiality, integrity, and authentication. You can read more here: https://nvlpubs.nist.gov/nistpubs/SpecialPublications/NIST.SP.800-77r1.pdf.

Although you have a choice of headers, the most effective option when setting up IPsec is to use the ESP protocol. Let's see what's involved in this process, next.

Encapsulating the security payloads

The ESP protocol provides data confidentiality and optional authentication of data packets between hosts. The ESP protocol provides the following services:

- Assures data integrity

- Provides host authentication

- Protects against replay attacks

- Ensures data confidentiality

ESP is a robust protocol that has many of the same field values as the AH protocol, as shown in the following screenshot:

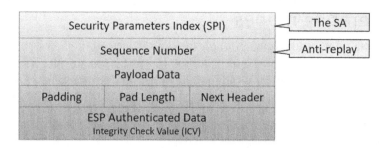

Figure 9.13 – The ESP header

The field values are outlined as follows:

- The SPI is the SA used to differentiate the various traffic streams using specific encryption algorithms and policies.

- The sequence number is a counter of the packet sequence that protects against a replay attack.

- The payload data contains data from the original IP packet. Depending on the payload, the length can vary.

- **Padding** and **Pad Length** are fields that are optionally used, as some encryption algorithms require data to be padded in order to have a certain block size.

- **Next Header** indicates the header that is following the IPsec ESP.

- The AH ICV is the ICV that authenticates the source and verifies the integrity of the payload.

You can use the ESP protocol to ensure confidentiality along with authentication. While authentication is optional when using ESP, it is recommended as it provides an additional layer of protection against attacks.

The ESP protocol will authenticate all immutable field values in the IP header, along with any protocols in Layers 4-7 of the OSI model. The ESP protocol can be used in either transport or tunnel operating modes.

> **Important note**
> In some cases, you will see ESP used alongside AH, which will be dependent on how IPsec is implemented.

When using IPsec, a network administrator can select either transport or tunnel mode, which will determine how packets are handled during transit. Let's see how each method works.

Using operating modes

When using IPsec, data must travel through various devices on the LAN—such as routers and firewalls—before heading out to the internet. In most cases, devices will need to see the source and destination IP address so that they can route the packets.

IPsec has two operating modes: transport and tunnel. The mode used will depend on which options the network administrator selected and where on the network the IPsec packets must travel. Both modes are outlined here:

- **Transport mode** is appropriate when a device such as a router must see the IP addresses and/or use **network address translation (NAT)** on the data packets.

- **Tunnel mode** is commonly used between two gateways when traveling over the internet.

When the IP packet is prepared for transit using either transport or tunnel mode, IPsec will modify the packets differently. First, let's see how IPsec treats the AH protocol in each mode.

Transforming the AH protocol

As shown in the following screenshot, IPsec will authenticate the data according to the operating mode:

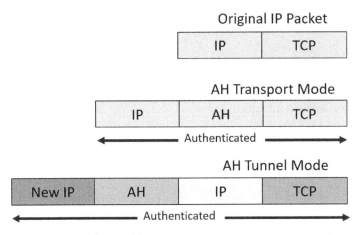

Figure 9.14 – Using the AH protocol in transport or tunnel mode

When using the AH protocol, data will be transformed according to the mode, as follows:

- **Transport mode**: IPsec will authenticate the payload and any immutable header fields, along with any IPv6 extensions.

- **Tunnel mode**: The authentication header and the IP header are authenticated. IPsec will place a new IP header around the entire packet and treat the original IP packet as data. IPsec will then authenticate the data payload and select the fields of the new IP header.

Next, we'll examine the ESP protocol.

Protecting the ESP protocol

As shown in the following screenshot, IPsec will authenticate and encrypt according to the operating mode:

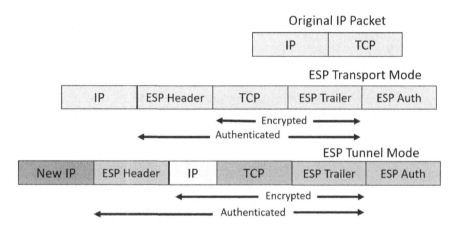

Figure 9.15 – Using the ESP protocol in transport or tunnel mode

When using the ESP protocol with authentication, data will be transformed according to the mode, as follows:

- **Transport mode**: IPsec will encrypt the payload and any IPv6 extensions along with authenticating the payload, but not the IP header.

- **Tunnel mode**: IPsec will encrypt and authenticate the inner IP packet. In tunnel mode, you will see the ESP protocol followed by the IP header, and then the payload. At this point, IPsec will place a new IP header around the entire packet and then treat the original IP packet as data.

How the two modes are used will depend on the data path. For example, if the data starts in a private network, the IP packet might start out in transport mode. After passing through the router and NAT device, IPsec can then add a header to be in tunnel mode as the packet travels across the insecure internet. Once safely in a private network on the other side, the device can remove the tunnel mode header and deliver the payload.

Another component of IPsec is the DH key agreement protocol. Let's see how this is used.

Generating a shared secret key with DH

If you recall, in *Chapter 5*, *Dissecting Asymmetric Encryption*, in the *Realizing the need for asymmetric encryption* section, we learned about the DH algorithm. We discussed how it was developed to address the issue of obtaining the same **shared secret** (**SS**) key during a data transaction.

When using the DH algorithm in IPsec, the host is configured to select a DH group, which is then used during phase 1 of the IPsec VPN.

There are many DH groups that define the type of encryption along with the key length that is used during the DH key-generating process. For example, you might see a list of groups as follows:

```
DH Group 15 (3072-bit)
DH Group 16 (4096-bit)
DH Group 17 (6144-bit)
```

Figure 9.16 – Partial listing of DH groups

The group selection may be dependent upon the device vendor, for example, the XYZ firewall company might state that they only support the following: DH Group 1, DH Group 2, and DH Group 5.

According to *NIST SP 800-77 revision 1*, DH groups 14-21 will provide the most security. In general, a higher group number will provide improved security; however, using a higher group number will be more resource-intensive. Therefore, a company will need to balance the need for security with the available resources.

One of the primary reasons DH is used is to provide **perfect forward secrecy** (**PFS**). Let's explore this concept, next.

Ensuring PFS

When encrypting traffic using symmetric encryption, both sides must share the same secret key. There are two main ways to exchange the key, outlined as follows:

- Using *encryption*, with asymmetric algorithms such as **Rivest-Shamir-Adleman** (**RSA**) or **Elliptic Curve Cryptography** (**ECC**)

- Using *key agreement*, via the DH process

If the process uses encryption, the parties will generate a public key private key pair, and then use asymmetric encryption to securely exchange the shared secret key.

During the course of exchanging encrypted traffic, it is essential to protect a server's private key. If disclosed, an attacker can have access to the transmitted data, which poses a serious risk to data security. However, cyber criminals work hard to get into systems and steal information, and have created several malware variants that can steal both private keys and digital certificates.

The solution: use PFS, as it provides assurance that no one can compromise the session keys, even if someone obtains the server's private key.

Unlike using asymmetric encryption to exchange an SS key, DH is a *key agreement* protocol. The protocol is designed to have each party generate the same SS key that will be used in a session between two parties.

PFS generates a unique session key for every session a user initiates by using the DH key exchange.

If a hacker is able to obtain a single session key, this only affects data exchanged in the current session protected by that specific key.

To enable PFS, both the client and the server must use a cipher suite that employs the DH key exchange.

To create a more secure VPN tunnel, it is mostly recommended to enable PFS when configuring an IPsec VPN tunnel.

When using IPsec, the AH and ESP protocols depend on cryptographic techniques and algorithms using asymmetric and symmetric encryption. As a result, key management is an integral part of IPsec, as outlined next.

Managing the keys using IKE

IPsec requires cryptographic keys to secure traffic. Depending on the organization, the keys can be managed manually or by using IKE, which automates the process.

If IPsec is being implemented on two internal servers on a LAN, a network administrator might use a manual method of managing and configuring the keys. However, for most implementations, using an automated method is a more efficient option. Let's see how this works.

Automating the process

IPsec uses IKE to securely exchange the keys between two hosts, and this is comprised of two protocols: **Internet Security Association and Key Management Protocol** (**ISAKMP**) and Oakley. The two protocols work together to provide the following services:

- ISAKMP authenticates hosts, manages session keys, and coordinates SAs.

- Oakley employs the DH key agreement protocol to exchange keys between hosts.

When setting up the SAs in IPsec, IKE has two phases, outlined as follows:

- **Phase 1** authenticates the IPsec peers using digital certificates, asymmetric encryption, or **pre-shared keys** (**PSKs**), and then prepares a secure channel in order to generate the shared keys.

- **Phase 2** will negotiate the security services and create the SA on both peers.

During the course of an IPsec transaction, IPsec may recreate a SA or generate new DH keys, which is done to improve the security of the transaction.

When setting up an IPsec profile, a network administrator may be able to choose from **IKE version 1** (**IKEv1**) or **IKE version 2** (**IKEv2**). Where possible, NIST suggests using IKEv2 as this offers enhanced security and is more scalable. In addition, IKEv2 has built-in NAT traversal, which provides a way for packets to move through NAT firewalls more easily.

Now that you understand the components necessary for IPsec, let's see what's involved in creating an IPsec profile.

Setting up an IPsec profile

When setting up an IPsec VPN, a network administrator has several options when creating a profile, as shown in the following screenshot:

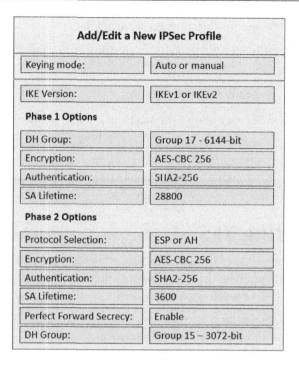

Figure 9.17 – Creating an IPsec profile

Let's step through the options, as follows:

- **Add/Edit a New IPSec Profile**

    Keying mode can be automatic or manual.

    IKE Version can be IKEv1 or IKEv2.

- **Phase 1 Options**

    - The **DH group** is selected according to the approved groups.

    - **Encryption** is the method used when securing data.

    - The **Authentication** algorithm is for when using either the AH or ESP with authentication.

    - **SA Lifetime** is generally listed in seconds. This can be any value; however, NIST recommends 86400 seconds (24 hours).

- **Phase 2 Options**

    - **Protocol Selection** refers to the protocol used to secure the data. This can be either ESP or AH.

- **Encryption** is the method used when securing data.

- The **Authentication** algorithm is for when using either the AH or ESP with authentication.

- **SA Lifetime** is generally listed in seconds.

- **Perfect Forward Secrecy** allows the administrator to define whether or not PFS is enabled.

- For **DH Group**, a DH group is selected according to the approved groups.

In addition to IPsec, another widely used VPN is a TLS VPN, as outlined next.

Understanding TLS

For many years, consumers have been conducting transactions on the internet. Up until recently, a website could get away with not having a secure connection. However, most consumers nowadays insist on some form of encryption to protect against malicious activity.

Secure Sockets Layer (**SSL**)/TLS-based VPNs have been around since the early 1990s. Netscape (which later became Firefox) developed this protocol to secure traffic while on the internet. Originally known as SSL, this method was widely recognized as a way to secure traffic between clients and web browsers. The protocol has improved over the years in the following ways:

- SSL 2.0-SSL 3.0 represent early versions of the protocol. SSL 3.0 is no longer used.

- TLS 1.0 is essentially an upgrade of SSL 1.0; although the protocol was to be deprecated in 2020, you may still see this version in use.

- TLS 1.1 was released in 2006. TLS 1.1 was also to be deprecated in 2020; however you may still see this version in use.

- TLS 1.2 was released in 2008 and offered improved algorithms for authentication, along with modified cipher suites.

- TLS 1.3 was released in 2018 and removed support for obsolete or insecure features such as compression, reduced the cipher suites to four, and mandated the use of PFS.

> **Important note**
>
> Because of security weaknesses in SSL, the use of an SSL VPN has been deprecated since 2015; therefore, for our discussion, we will focus on TLS.

A TLS VPN provides data protection for the upper layers (Layers 5-7) of the OSI model while transmitting across the internet. A TLS VPN can be used to secure connections for protocols such as the following:

- **HyperText Transfer Protocol (HTTP)**
- **File Transfer Protocol (FTP)**
- **Simple Mail Transport Protocol (SMTP)**

TLS is comprised of two layers of protocols that sit between the application layer and the transport layer, as shown in the following screenshot:

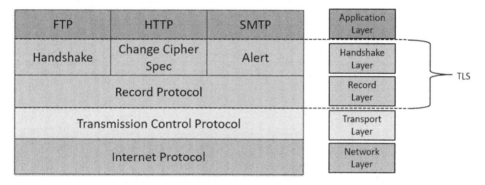

Figure 9.18 – The TLS protocol stack

Within the TLS layer there are two protocol sublayers, as follows:

- **Handshake protocols**: These authenticate the peers, establish the cryptographic parameters of the session, and exchange the key.
- **Record protocol**: This encrypts and/or authenticates data transmitted between the client and the server.

As shown in *Figure 9.19*, the TLS protocol moves through a process that begins with the client requesting to make a connection with the server, using a TCP three-way handshake. The three-way handshake is then followed by the TLS handshake protocol. Once the handshake is complete, the Record protocol begins to exchange data, as illustrated in the following diagram:

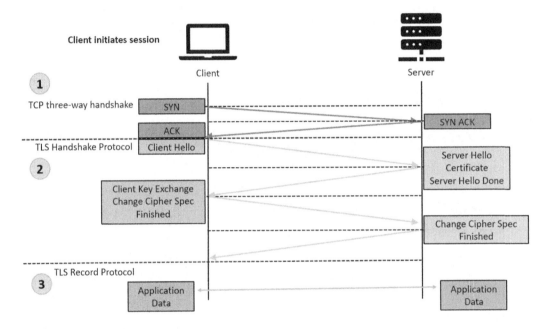

Figure 9.19 – The TLS process

So that you have a better understanding of what goes on during a TLS session, we'll take a look at what happens in both the TLS handshake and Record protocols.

Let's start with the handshake protocols.

Understanding the handshake protocols

Within the TLS handshake layer are three handshake protocols that work together to negotiate and prepare a session.

The three protocols are outlined as follows:

- The **handshake protocol** is responsible for exchanging the session parameters between the hosts.

- The **change cipher spec protocol** is responsible for changing the ciphering strategies.

- The **alert protocol** is responsible for signaling an error, closure, warning, or other alert.

In this section, we'll evaluate each of the three protocols involved in preparing a session. Let's start with the handshake protocol.

Completing a handshake

When beginning a session with a web server using TLS, the two hosts must complete a handshake prior to exchanging any data. As expected, a handshake is the most complex part of TLS as it requires both parties to agree on the terms of the session and must be completed before any application data is transmitted.

I'll show you some examples in Wireshark. If you would like to follow along, you can obtain a TLS 1.3 packet capture at `https://github.com/wireshark/wireshark/blob/master/test/captures/tls13-rfc8446.pcap` (`tls13rfc8446.pcapng`) and open it in Wireshark.

> **Important note**
>
> Make sure you have the latest version of Wireshark for the dissectors to render the TLS version properly. However, in some cases, Wireshark might not be able to display the correct version in the frame details.

The TLS process starts with the `Client Hello` phase. To see an example of the `Client Hello` message, go to frame 1 and expand the `Client Hello` message under the `Handshake Protocol` header, as shown in the following screenshot:

```
˅ Handshake Protocol: Client Hello
    Handshake Type: Client Hello (1)
    Length: 229
    Version: TLS 1.2 (0x0303)
    Random: 2635fafc16c49a3e997ef714c303806dc8dbf634a2005b0e0186521c4ad6f9df
    Session ID Length: 32
    Session ID: 23c3a84ca631f3a948d15d929c972e00dded0857f2a00fbadd56175c4e362b84
    Cipher Suites Length: 36
  ˃ Cipher Suites (18 suites)
    Compression Methods Length: 1
  ˃ Compression Methods (1 method)
    Extensions Length: 120
  ˃ Extension: renegotiation_info (len=1)
```

Figure 9.20 – TLS Client Hello

The Client Hello message will start the request, which includes the following fields:

- Version is the TLS version requested by the client. For example, you might see the following version listed: TLS 1.2.

- Random will be a string of random text. For example, you might see the following: cd3815dc6534c019c169abc12.

- Session ID is used if the client has a specific ID. If not used, the field is left blank.

- Cipher Suites represents the client-supported cryptographic algorithms used to complete key exchange, authentication, and encryption.

- Compression Methods indicates the client's desired compression algorithms.

In addition, a Client Hello message may have extensions.

In Frame 1, if you expand the Cipher Suites field, you will see a list of ciphers, starting with the client's top choice listed first, as shown in the following screenshot:

```
˅ Cipher Suites (18 suites)
    Cipher Suite: TLS_AES_128_GCM_SHA256 (0x1301)
    Cipher Suite: TLS_AES_256_GCM_SHA384 (0x1302)
    Cipher Suite: TLS_CHACHA20_POLY1305_SHA256 (0x1303)
    Cipher Suite: TLS_ECDHE_ECDSA_WITH_AES_128_GCM_SHA256 (0xc02b)
    Cipher Suite: TLS_ECDHE_RSA_WITH_AES_128_GCM_SHA256 (0xc02f)
    Cipher Suite: TLS_ECDHE_ECDSA_WITH_AES_256_GCM_SHA384 (0xc02c)
    Cipher Suite: TLS_ECDHE_RSA_WITH_AES_256_GCM_SHA384 (0xc030)
    Cipher Suite: TLS_ECDHE_ECDSA_WITH_CHACHA20_POLY1305_SHA256 (0xcca9)
    Cipher Suite: TLS_ECDHE_RSA_WITH_CHACHA20_POLY1305_SHA256 (0xcca8)
```

Figure 9.21 – A list of supported cipher suites

The next phase will be the Server Hello phase, which has the same fields as the Client Hello phase. However, this will provide a response to the client request with the server capabilities and algorithms. The server will also send their signed X.509v3 **certificate**. At that point, the server will send a Server Hello Done message and then wait to hear from the client.

The client will send a Client Key Exchange message (which holds the pre-master secret) to the server. From the pre-master secret, the server then creates the master secret and session keys used to encrypt the traffic between the client and server.

The client will also send the Change Cipher Spec message, letting the server know the client will use any new session keys. The client then will send a Client Finished message.

As we have seen, a handshake creates a *session* between a client and a server. Let's take a look at just what's involved when referencing a session.

Creating a session

During the handshake protocol, the server will create a session to preserve state information. A TLS session is created with the security parameters required for the secure transfer of information. The session maintains the state information to prevent the expensive negotiation of moving through the handshake phase again.

Within the session, the security parameters are defined and can be used with multiple connections, as shown in the following figure:

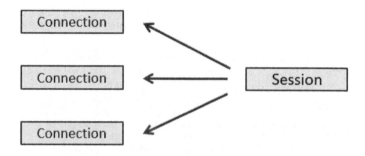

Figure 9.22 – One session with multiple connections

A connection is a relationship between a client and a server. Each connection has a separate key. A connection can be short-lived and closed—for example, if there is a timeout. However, the session can be resumed using another connection.

There is an option for a client and a server to resume a previous session by using its session ID. At that point, a full handshake process is not needed.

Throughout a TLS transaction, you will see the change cipher spec protocol, as discussed next.

Grasping the change cipher spec protocol

At any time after a handshake, either a client or a server can send a `change cipher spec` message, which notifies the other party that the sender wants to change to a new set of keys.

Once the other party receives this message, this signals new ciphering strategies.

Periodically, there will be an issue during the data transaction. At that point, either host can send an alert. Let's see what might cause either party to issue an alert.

Using an alert

An alert is a message that indicates to the peer a change in status or an error condition. The alert can signal a wide variety of alerts to notify the peer of both normal and error conditions. Alerts can notify us of the following:

- A handshake failure.

- The connection is closed.

- An invalid message has been received.

- A message cannot be decrypted.

- The user has canceled the operation.

If an alert is due to a fatal condition, this results in the immediate termination of the connection.

Once the handshake is complete and everything goes well, the two parties can exchange data as we move into the Record protocol, as outlined next.

Dissecting the Record protocol

In the Record protocol, all messages are encrypted. Prior to sending the application data, TLS readies the data, as shown in the following figure:

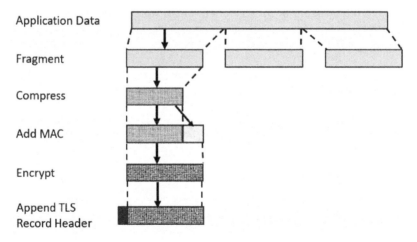

Figure 9.23 – Transforming data in the Record protocol

TLS will transform the data in the following manner:

1. If the data block is greater than 2^14 bytes, the data must be fragmented into smaller blocks.

2. The data is compressed using a lossless data compression algorithm.

3. TLS generates a **message authentication code** (**MAC**) and appends that to the compressed data.

4. The block of data and the MAC are encrypted.

5. The TLS record header is then applied.

Once all the steps are completed, the data is then transmitted. Once it is received, the reverse occurs, and the decrypted data is presented to the host.

As you can see, there is a lot that goes on when encrypting data using TLS.

Summary

Nowadays, much of our data is protected using some form of encryption. A VPN provides a secure tunnel to transmit data over an insecure network. In this chapter, we defined the meaning of a VPN and outlined some examples. We saw how consumers can secure data using OpenVPN or browser-based VPNs. We also saw how network administrators can use an SSH VPN for remote configuration and learned how PuTTY provides an easy method to use SSH on a Windows machine.

We then outlined the elements of an IPsec VPN. We examined the authentication header and discovered the encapsulating security payload, and saw what's involved when selecting an operating mode. We saw the importance of the IKE process and an example of what an administrator might see when setting up an IPsec profile on a device. We then finished up with a discussion of TLS. We saw what happens in both the TLS Record and handshake protocols by covering the handshake, change cipher spec, and alert protocols; and, once the handshake is done, we saw how TLS protects data in the Record protocol.

In the next chapter, we'll outline attacks on encrypted data that can threaten the effectiveness of cryptographic techniques. We'll then learn how a **public key infrastructure** (**PKI**) can also be a target and can suffer from attacks such as a TLS strip, along with other exploits. Finally, we'll review the fact that current encryption algorithms have been in existence for decades. However, we'll see how quantum computing may be able to decrypt data with ease and render current encryption algorithms obsolete. We'll then see how scientists are designing stronger algorithms to keep apace with technology, to avoid this threat.

Questions

Now, it's time to check your knowledge. Select the best response to the following questions and then check your answers, found in the *Assessment* section at the end of the book:

1. _____ was the first VPN and can work with almost any operating system; however, it is not secure and should be avoided.

   a. PPTP

   b. L2TP

   c. SSTP

   d. IKE

2. _____ is a technology used to securely access remote hosts. When using this type of VPN, once the client and server are connected, you will interface with the host using the CLI.

   a. PPTP

   b. ISAKMP

   c. IKE

   d. SSH

3. The _____ protocol provides data confidentiality and optional authentication of data packets between hosts.

   a. PPTP

   b. ESP

   c. AH

   d. IKE

4. When traveling in _____ mode, IPsec will encrypt only the data portion of each packet yet leave the header unencrypted.

   a. tunnel

   b. IKE

   c. PFS

   d. transport

5. In order to protect against a malicious actor gaining access into a system and stealing a server's private key, a network administrator should use _____.

   a. PPTP

   b. ISAKMP

   c. PFS

   d. AH

6. IPsec requires cryptographic keys to secure traffic. Depending on the organization, the keys can be managed manually or by using _____.

   a. PPTP

   b. IKE

   c. PFS

   d. AH

7. Within the TLS layer, the _____ protocols authenticate the peers, establish the cryptographic parameters of the session, and exchange the key.

   a. handshake

   b. DH

   c. Record

   d. ISAKMP

8. Within the TLS layer, the _____ protocol uses the secret key established in the handshake protocol to protect communication between the client and the server.

   a. handshake

   b. DH

   c. Record

   d. ISAKMP

Further reading

Please refer to the following links for more information:

- To obtain a browser extension for HTTPS Everywhere, visit `https://www.eff.org/https-everywhere`.

- To see detailed instructions on how to set up a VPN using Windows 98, visit `https://web.invest.yale.edu/VPN/VPNSetupforWindows98.htm`.

- To read more on the *Security of Interactive and Automated Access Management Using SSH*, visit `https://nvlpubs.nist.gov/nistpubs/ir/2015/NIST.IR.7966.pdf`.

- To step though the process of generating a key pair in SSH, visit `https://upcloud.com/community/tutorials/use-ssh-keys-authentication/`.

- Visit *NIST SP 800-77 revision 1* at `https://nvlpubs.nist.gov/nistpubs/SpecialPublications/NIST.SP.800-77r1.pdf`.

- For an overview of IPsec, visit `https://networkdirection.net/articles/network-theory/ipsecbasics/`.

- To read about SSL and TLS, visit `https://dev.to/techschoolguru/a-complete-overview-of-ssl-tls-and-its-cryptographic-system-36pd`.

- To learn more about IKE, visit IKE **Request for Comments (RFC)** at `https://tools.ietf.org/html/rfc2409`.

- To see the differences between IKEv1 and IKEv2, visit `https://www.kareemccie.com/2016/12/differences-between-ikev1-and-ikev2.html`.

- For an article on outlining the details of an IPsec VPN, visit `https://www.juniper.net/documentation/en_US/junos/topics/topic-map/security-ipsec-vpn-overview.html`.

- Visit `https://www.thesslstore.com/blog/explaining-ssl-handshake/` to learn more about the TLS handshake.

- Visit `https://tools.ietf.org/html/rfc5246` to learn more on TLS.

- For another example of TLS 1.3 go to `https://www.cloudshark.org/captures/a044d58b77aa` and download the `tls_1_3.pcapng` file, and open it in Wireshark.

- To learn what's new in TLS 1.3, visit `https://cloudshark.io/articles/examples-of-tls-1-3/`.

10
Protecting Cryptographic Techniques

Encryption and hashing algorithms, along with cryptographic tools and techniques, are designed to enhance the security of our data and systems. As with many other things, there is always the threat that someone can disrupt this security. This can occur if a malicious actor launches an attack on the very methods designed to protect us. In this chapter, we'll learn that it's essential to protect our cryptographic techniques, given that there are many threats that exist today.

First, we'll take a look at a number of attacks, including brute-force and password attacks, all designed to alter the integrity of our data or a system. We'll also see how there are tools readily available for the malicious actor and will take a brief look at Kali Linux. We will then outline an example of what happens when a less secure protocol is used, as we cover the deficiencies in the **Wired Equivalency Protocol** (WEP).

We'll also outline the importance of trust when exchanging data. Specifically, we'll recognize how the **Public Key Infrastructure** (**PKI**) is a critical component that enables entities to securely communicate with one another. We'll then outline how this infrastructure can be attacked, as we cover some methods to negate the trust, such as stealing certificates or launching a denial-of-service attack. Finally, we'll see how advances in technology, such as quantum computing, will require the use of quantum-resistant algorithms to encrypt and secure our data.

In this chapter, we're going to cover the following main topics:

- Recognizing cryptographic attacks

- Attacking the infrastructure

- Influence of quantum computing

Recognizing cryptographic attacks

We rely on cryptographic techniques and algorithms to secure our systems. However, we must be aware of the possibility of an attack on encryption protocols and techniques that can result in our data being compromised.

Over the years, there have been many documented attacks, some simple, some more complex. For example, early algorithms, such as mono-alphabetic ciphers, can easily be attacked using letter frequency analysis. However, as ciphers became more complex, the types of attacks also had to become more sophisticated.

In this section, we'll discuss brute-force, password, and **Man-in-The-Middle** (**MiTM**) attacks, along with a brief look at some less-known methods used to compromise a system. In addition, we'll discuss Kali Linux, a powerful suite of tools that can be used to attack cryptographic techniques. We'll also see how WEP, an early wireless encryption protocol, was a weak cipher that allowed a malicious actor to obtain the key and decode the data stream.

Let's start with a review of some cryptographic attacks.

Comparing various attacks

When trying to gain access to either data or a system that is protected using encryption, there are many different types of attacks. Let's take a look at some of these, starting with a brute-force attack.

Attacking with brute force

Imagine trying to break down a door. Depending on the door, you might need to resort to using methods with a sledge hammer, your foot, or even a battering ram. Similar to trying to break down a door, a brute-force attack attempts to break the encryption to expose the plain text, by trying every possible key combination.

Using a brute-force attack can be resource-intensive. For example, the **Data Encryption Standard (DES)** uses a key size of 56-bits. That equates to 2^{56}, or 72 quadrillion possible keys. While it may seem improbable that a 56-bit key could be derived using a brute-force attack, this was done in 1997. The deliberate attack on DES was done in response to a challenge made by **Rivest, Shamir and Adleman (RSA)** security. This was achieved by an individual in Salt Lake City using only a PC. He was able to brute-force the key after only going through approximately 25% of the key combinations. The lesson here is, if a longer key is used to encrypt data, a brute-force attack is more difficult. However, this could still be possible, given enough time and processing.

Another way to attack a cryptographic safeguard is by using a MiTM attack, as we'll see next.

Being an MiTM

An MiTM attack is when a malicious actor positions themself in the middle of a communication channel and is able to intercept all traffic. This is generally done by using either a spoofing or cache poisoning strategy, such as one of the following:

- **Domain Name System (DNS) cache poisoning** sends bogus records to a DNS resolver. As a result, when a victim requests an **Internet Protocol (IP)** address for a website, the DNS server will send the wrong IP address. The bogus IP address will redirect traffic to the malicious actor's IP address instead of the (actual) web server's IP address.

- **Address Resolution Protocol (ARP) spoofing** transmits spoofed ARP messages out on the local area network. The spoofed messages falsely report a malicious actor's **Media Access Control (MAC)** address as being the victim's address. Similar to a DNS cache poisoning attack, this will redirect traffic to the malicious actor instead of the victim's (MAC address) machine.

- **MAC address spoofing** will modify the MAC address on the malicious actor's network interface card so that it matches the MAC address on the victim's machine. Once done, the traffic will be directed to both the victim and the malicious actor.

By using any of these attacks, when a device needs to deliver a message to the victim, it will instead send the message to the malicious actor.

Let's now outline the steps taken to spoof a MAC address.

Spoofing a MAC address

When spoofing a MAC address, the malicious actor must first determine the MAC address of the victim. Once determined, the next step is to modify the settings in the adapter properties to match the victim's MAC address, as shown in the following screenshot:

Figure 10.1 – Adapter properties

As shown in the following diagram, the malicious actor's real MAC address has been modified so that it is the same as the victim's MAC address:

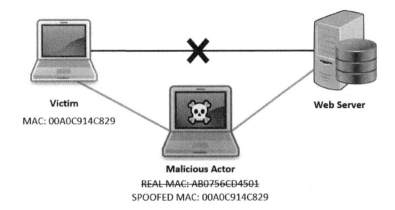

Figure 10.2 – An MiTM attack

Once modified, whenever traffic is sent to the victim, it will also be sent to the malicious actor as well.

In addition to an MiTM attack, another attack is where a malicious actor launches a password attack by using a technique called pass the hash. Let's discuss this next.

Passing the hash

When you create a password, a system stores the value as a hash instead of plain text. This is so that if anyone were to get a hold of the password files on a system, they wouldn't be able to see the passwords and use them to access protected resources. Because of this, another type of attack uses the *hash* of a password instead of the actual password, in an attack called 'pass the hash'.

Using pass the hash is possible in operating systems that use **New Technology Local Area Network Management (NTLM)** authentication. NTLM uses a **Message Digest 4 (MD4)** hash algorithm to generate a hash of the password. The attack is possible because of a vulnerability in the NTLM whereby the password hash remains the same until the user changes their password.

Important note

To see what an MD4 hash looks like, go to this website, `https://en.toolpage.org/tool/md4`, where you can convert a password to an MD4 hash as follows:

Password: `orangetigerkittens`

MD4 hash: `8697440e4410fb944e4245798a7b52b3`

The attack begins by the malicious actor obtaining a username and password hash. Then, when attempting to log in to a system, the server will send an authentication challenge. The malicious actor must respond appropriately in order to gain access to the system, as shown in the following diagram:

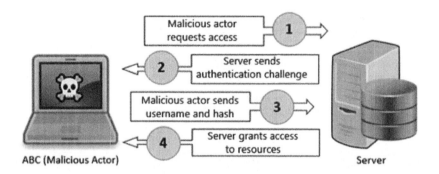

Figure 10.3 – A pass the hash attack

The process for pass the hash goes as follows:

1. **Malicious actor**: Hi. I'm ABC, and I would like access to your resources.

2. **Server**: Okay ABC, we'll need you to prove who you are. Your challenge is to encrypt the word SHARKPUPS by using the DES and an MD4 hash of your password.

3. **Malicious actor**: Okay, here you go: fvfnY5Ppl221sU/UTSHDFg==.

4. **Server**: Perfect! You are granted access!

Many of the attacks we see are common. However, there are also some less-known, advanced attacks that can compromise a system and threaten the effectiveness of cryptographic techniques, as we'll see next.

Using advanced techniques

A determined malicious actor may go to extremes to access data. For example, they might use a side-channel attack, which is not a brute-force attack. Instead, it breaks a cryptosystem by employing a sideways or indirect approach. The method works by observing or gathering the electrical signals, power surges, or sounds that a digital device discharges when someone is inputting data. This is similar to a safe cracker using a stethoscope to hear the faint clicks when hitting the correct number in a combination safe. Once obtained, the malicious actor uses the signals to gain access to the data.

Another attack uses differential cryptanalysis to obtain the plain text, which relies on the *differences* in the encrypted and plain text to determine the key. This is also known as a chosen plain text attack, as the malicious actor would need to submit plain text to be encrypted (without any knowledge of the key), and then use both plain and encrypted text to derive the key.

As you can see, several attacks exist against cryptographic techniques. The reality is that a malicious actor most likely has several tools with which to launch an attack. One tool that provides a suite of attack tools is called Kali Linux. Let's take a look at this next.

Using Kali Linux

Over the years, there have been numerous attacks on encryption and hash algorithms. Malicious actors have a wide variety of freely available tools at their disposal. One such tool is called Kali Linux. Formerly called *Backtrack*, this Debian-based Linux distribution has hundreds of tools, including tools to attack encryption and cryptographic techniques.

To get a copy of Kali Linux that is premade to work in a virtual machine, you can visit the following link: `https://www.osboxes.org/kali-linux/`. Once in Kali Linux, you can select from one of several tools, including the following:

- **Hashfind**: This tool will search files to locate a given value in a hash table.
- **Httpsscanner**: This tool will scan a web server to check for SSL misconfigurations.
- **Morxcrack**: This tool will run a dictionary attack on **Content Management System (CMS)** salted passwords.
- **Pybozocrack**: This tool will run an attack on MD5 hashed passwords.
- **John the Ripper**: This is a suite of tools designed to discover the plain text passwords that have been hashed, using algorithms such as MD5 and **Secure Hash Algorithm (SHA)**.

While Kali Linux has a wide range of tools, it may not be possible to obtain a password, as some methods to secure a password are better than others. The fact is, the strength of a crypto system is gauged by how resilient it is to an attack.

In the next section, we'll take a closer look at a weak encryption algorithm, WEP, and what faults made it insecure.

Cracking WEP

In the late 1990s, the 802.11 standard (Wi-Fi) started to show up on everyone's radar. However, on its own, Wi-Fi is not secure. Unencrypted Wi-Fi traffic can be captured by using a packet sniffer (such as Wireshark) and then the attacker can view the plain text transmission.

Because of the fact that Wi-Fi was insecure, scientists quickly sought ways to secure the protocol. The WEP was designed to be as secure as an encrypted 'wired' connection and provided an early way to encrypt wireless data transmissions.

When encrypting wireless communications, we use a stream cipher, which encrypts the data one bit or one byte at a time. Stream ciphers use a single shared key to encrypt the data. Because it is a stream cipher, we require an **initialization vector (IV)**, which is a 'dummy block' to start the key stream generator.

WEP used **Ron's Code 4 (RC4)**, and soon after WEP was standardized in 1997, issues with the protocol became apparent. Some of these issues included the following:

- The IV is only 24 bits. Because it is so short, the IV must be repeated during the data transmission.

- The IV remains the same throughout the transmission and is sent in plain text.

- The IV is part of the key, as it is added to the beginning of the encryption key.

- By capturing the IV, and enough of the data stream, a malicious actor can obtain the key by using software, such as Kali Linux or Aircrack, that can recover the key.

- Once the key is derived, the malicious actor can decrypt the data stream.

By using Wireshark while capturing traffic, we can examine the WEP parameters. As shown in the following screenshot, we see a screenshot of a frame:

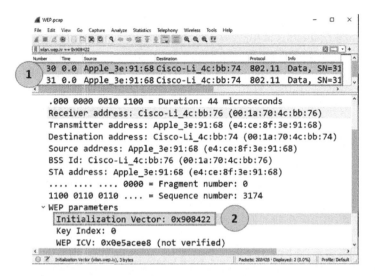

Figure 10.4 – The initialization vector in WEP

Within the frame are the `WEP parameters`:

- The IV, which is a 24-bit binary number. As shown in the preceding screenshot, this is represented as a 6-character hexadecimal number: `908422`.

- The **Key Index**: 0, which is the default that is set for the **Access Point** (**AP**). The default for a Windows client would be 1.

- The **Integrity Check Value** (**ICV**), which is used to validate that the data was not altered in transit. This value as shown is an 8-character hexadecimal number: `0e5acee8`.

What is important here are two issues as shown in the preceding screenshot:

1. Here we see two frames listed at the top of the filtered packet list, which shows where the IV was repeated during the transmission.

2. Here we see the IV transmitted in plain text.

WEP was an early Wi-Fi encryption algorithm. Although insecure, and ultimately deprecated, there were some lessons that were derived from using WEP. One is that you should never reuse the IV, as it can be used to derive the key, and the IV should not be sent in plain text.

As illustrated, it's important to select the most secure algorithm to protect your data. One key reason is that a malicious actor can launch an attack with freely available tools, such as those in Kali Linux. In addition to attacks on various cryptographic protocols, we also have to be aware of someone disrupting the integrity of the PKI as well. Let's take a look at this next.

Attacking the infrastructure

Most cryptosystems require a framework or infrastructure in order to effectively secure data. One infrastructure that enables all parties to communicate securely with one another is the PKI. PKI comprises the processes, elements, and algorithms that are required to securely send and receive data.

In addition to individual protocols, PKI can also suffer from attacks. In this section, we'll see how the PKI can provide the trust we need when making transactions on the internet. We'll then see how the PKI can be a target and can suffer from attacks such as an SSL/TLS strip, using stolen certificates to distribute malware, and denial-of-service attacks.

Let's start with a discussion on how the PKI guarantees trust.

Guaranteeing trust

When interacting with a company, it's important that you work with someone you can trust. If dealing with a traditional brick and mortar entity, you might look for a sign that shows an excellent rating from the **Better Business Bureau**. Or, if shopping online, you might look for a large number of favorable reviews listed by the vendor's name. This trust helps us to more confidently enter into business with the company.

On the internet, when we visit a website, we need to have some type of trust before exchanging data. This is achieved through the PKI, which generates a digital certificate to securely distribute keys between a server (such as a web server) and a client. PKI uses a **trusted third party** (**TTP**), also called a **Certificate Authority** (**CA**), that generates a signed certificate to ensure the authentication of each entity in a digital transaction. We learned about the PKI in Chapter 8, *Using a Public Key Infrastructure.*

The certificate is critical in a digital transaction on the internet. The CA uses the certificate to securely distribute the keys that are used to encrypt our transactions, so as to prevent prying eyes from accessing the contents of our data transmissions.

The overarching element of certificates in the PKI is the CA (or TTP). The trust is the glue that holds the framework together, so that we can confidently communicate in a nameless, faceless environment.

What happens when we can't assure that trust, because of an attack on the infrastructure? Let's explore this concept, next.

Violating trust

The CA is pivotal in the PKI framework. Because of the faith we have in the process, if someone were able to compromise that trust in some way, it would most likely lead to the exposure of sensitive data.

Over the years, there have been several attacks that have negated the value of the CA. These attacks have included SSL strips, theft of certificates, and denial-of-service attacks. Let's start with describing how an SSL/TLS strip works.

Performing an SSL/TLS strip

Whenever you are in a secure transaction on the internet, you will most likely be using SSL/TLS. **SSL** is **Secure Sockets Layer**, a protocol designed by *Netscape* in 1994 to provide secure transmissions over the internet. The protocol has advanced over the years, and most transactions now use **Transport Layer Security** (**TLS**), a newer protocol. Because of this evolution, and owing to the length of time that we used SSL, you may see the protocol defined as SSL/TLS. We learned about TLS in *Chapter 9, Exploring IPsec and TLS*.

Almost every legitimate company will use **Hypertext Transport Protocol** (**HTTP**) over an SSL/TLS connection that is identified as HTTPS, and that assures clients that there is a secure connection.

When a client begins a transaction with a web server, an SSL/TLS connection is established. This creates a **Virtual Private Network** (**VPN**), which allows secure encrypted transactions between a client and a server.

For the most part, an SSL/TLS connection is effective in securing data. However, on October 24, 2010, the world was introduced to *Firesheep*, which provided an easy way to launch an SSL strip attack. Let's take a look at this next.

Introducing Firesheep

Firesheep was an extension to the Firefox browser. Because Firesheep had a built-in packet sniffer, it could monitor and intercept communication streams, and take over someone's session while they were in a site.

Under normal circumstances, when logging in to an account such as Facebook, a client will first go to the landing page and log in to the site. Once Facebook determines that the client is a valid user, the server sends the client a cookie, which is a small text file that contains information related to the session. During that time, there was a good amount of unencrypted traffic, and the session cookies were sent in plain text. As a result, the attack was successful and easily accomplished.

Firesheep's main goal was to grab an unsuspecting victim's session cookies, so that they could gain access to a normally protected website, such as Twitter or Facebook. The extension would allow you to gain access to someone else's account by circumventing the password requirement.

Firesheep would work in the following manner:

1. A malicious actor would launch Firesheep on an open wireless network, for example, in a coffee shop.

2. Firesheep would quietly gather the cookies that were being transmitted as individuals were logging in to their sites.

3. Firesheep would then display the names of the clients that had logged in to their social media and other sites on the left-hand side of the screen.

4. To gain access to someone's site, such as Facebook or Twitter, the malicious actor would click on a name. The malicious actor would then be in that individual's site.

5. Meanwhile, the web page and all information would then be presented to the victim as if nothing was wrong.

Once the malicious actor gains access to someone's account, Firesheep will present the page as an HTTP page instead of an HTTPS page. As a result, Firesheep essentially *strips* the SSL/TLS connection.

For example, what you would see at the top of the browser once you get into someone's Twitter account would be as follows:

Figure 10.5 – An HTTP connection to Twitter.com

Firesheep is an MiTM attack that is a form of *session hijacking*, as a malicious actor obtains a victim's cookie and then takes over the session. Firesheep was effective because of several vulnerabilities. At the time, it was capable of taking over 26 different sites, including Amazon, Facebook, Twitter, and others. You can learn more about Firesheep at https://codebutler.com/2010/10/24/firesheep/.

Today there are tools within Kali Linux that can launch an SSL strip. However, because of advances in the protocols we use today, this attack is not as prevalent.

Another threat to the PKI is when someone fraudulently obtains a certificate, as we'll see next.

Stealing certificates

We briefly reviewed the PKI in *Chapter 1, Protecting Data in Motion or at Rest* under the *Managing keys using the PKI* section. In that section, we outlined how the PKI uses a CA (or TTP) to generate a digital certificate. The certificate is used to securely distribute cryptographic keys between two entities involved in a communication stream, such as a web server and a client.

During the course of browsing the internet, you will collect numerous certificates, as part of a normal data exchange in a secure connection. In **Certificate Manager**, generally found under the browser options, you will find a list of all of the certificates from various CAs, as shown in the following screenshot:

Figure 10.6 – Certificate Manager

We rely on the CA to provide the trust required when interacting on the internet. In addition, if we receive software updates, we need to be able to trust that the software is authentic. One way we are assured that the software is authentic and approved by the vendor is when it is signed with a digital certificate.

Called a *code signing certificate*, this certificate creates a digital signature to validate the following:

- Device drivers
- Application updates
- Documents
- Software packages

However, malicious actors are using code signing certificates to deliver malware. The malware attack begins by the malicious actor obtaining a certificate in some way. This can happen, as many times certificates are stored in several places, inside and outside of the protected network. Places include devices such as load balancers, firewalls, and proxy servers, which, if hacked, a malicious actor can access and obtain the certificate.

The malicious actor then pretends they are the CA and signs the malware to appear as if it is some type of trusted software or update. Because it is signed by using the CA's digital signature, this can trick a system into accepting malware. This type of attack is particularly dangerous, as almost every system, device, and computer relies on the trust of the code signing certificate that the software is safe to install and use.

In addition to using a certificate to deliver malware, there is also a threat of a denial-of-service attack against the CA, as outlined next.

Locking legitimate users out

When an SSL/TLS session begins, there is a process of establishing a secure connection. Beginning a session can be computationally intensive because of the various elements that occur during the handshake process.

If multiple requests to initiate an SSL/TLS session occur simultaneously, this can lead to the CA being overwhelmed. When done deliberately, this is called a **Denial-of-Service (DoS)** attack, which is designed to prevent legitimate users from being able to access the CA.

While there is a possibility that this type of attack can happen, over time there have been advances in technology. Safeguards include anti-DoS mechanisms that are essential in preventing attacks.

In addition to potential attacks to cryptographic protocols and the infrastructure, we must also be aware of the fact that advances in processing and computers in general can threaten the security of existing protocols.

The current encryption algorithms have been in existence for decades. Over the next few years, we'll begin to see advances in processing and the expanded use of quantum computers. Let's explore what this might mean to the security of existing cryptosystems next.

Influence of quantum computing

In the past decade, we started to see advancements in the field of quantum computing. Because of the sheer power of a quantum computer, some are concerned that our well-known cryptographic algorithms may not be able to withstand a brute-force attack using a quantum computer. In this section, we'll outline how quantum computing works, and see how the **National Institute of Standards and Technology (NIST)** is preparing to deal with this potential by selecting and standardizing *post-quantum* encryption algorithms.

Let's start by getting a better understanding of quantum computing.

Describing quantum computing

If we compare a classic and a quantum computer, there are distinct differences:

- A classic computer uses binary digits (or bits) and is based on transistors that have two states, on or off.

- A quantum computer uses quantum bits (or qubits), which can be in multiple states at the same time.

Quantum computing is based on the properties of quantum mechanics:

- **Superposition**: This is the ability to be in multiple states at the same time.

- **Entanglement**: This is when two particles are interrelated, in that if one changes, the other changes as well, no matter where in the universe the two particles exist.

- **Interference**: This is where a particle can be in more than one place at a time.

When properly designed, a quantum computer can process data faster than a classic computer. More specifically, quantum algorithms are much better at factoring prime numbers. If quantum technology becomes stable enough, this will ultimately affect the security of public key cryptography algorithms, such as RSA, mainly because public key cryptography relies on the fact that it is extremely difficult to factor prime numbers.

> **Important note**
>
> Learn more about quantum algorithms by visiting the following link:
> `https://www.nature.com/articles/s41598-020-62802-5`.

Over the last few decades, there has been more interest in developing quantum computers.

Currently, industry leaders, such as Google, IBM, Alibaba, and AT&T, are among a small group that are successfully working with quantum computing. These large companies are making headway in expanding the capacity of the qubits so that they can have practical applications.

Even with the strength and size of these companies, the computers themselves are not only expensive, but also limited in their capabilities. However, knowing that quantum computing can eventually be significantly more powerful than our existing systems has led to concerns regarding the strength of our current cryptographic algorithms. Let's discuss this next.

Implementing quantum-resistant algorithms

Quantum computing could potentially break current encryption protocols. However, the reality is that quantum computing won't become mainstream for the next few decades. For most of us, we will adjust to the changing requirements as they evolve.

Many scientists are confident that the **Advanced Encryption Standard** (**AES**) is quantum-resistant. Let's explore this concept next.

Using symmetric encryption

AES is a symmetric encryption algorithm that was standardized in the United States in 2001. Although a US government standard for encrypting and decrypting data, AES is used worldwide to secure data. It uses a single key (or secret key) and is a block cipher that can use a key length of either 128, 192, or 256 bits.

AES is a strong algorithm. Over the years, there have been a few discussions regarding the possibility of an attack against AES. For the most part, attacks against AES have had minimal success. Many scientists feel that when using a key length of 256 bits using 14 rounds, AES remains a solid algorithm and is quantum-resistant, at least for the foreseeable future.

However, while quantum computers are still in the development stage, scientists are actively working on developing public key cryptographic algorithms that can withstand the power of a quantum computer. Let's discuss the role of NIST in this effort.

Protecting public key cryptography

NIST has been actively seeking viable candidates for quantum-resistant cryptography since 2016. NIST's competition focuses on standardizing post-quantum public key encryption and digital signature algorithms.

NIST issued a call to the public to submit algorithms that are able to withstand the powerful computation abilities of a quantum computer. They received nearly 70 submissions and are narrowing the list down to a small number of viable candidates.

NIST will continue to evaluate these candidates over the next few years in varying applications and systems to test their strength. Tests will gauge their ability to encrypt data on a range of devices. Devices will include everything from supercomputers, mobile devices, and the Internet of Things to test their ability to encrypt with limited processing.

As we have seen, attacks against our cryptosystems are feasible. However, when properly designed and implemented, the standards are capable of protecting our data. However, as time moves forward, and technologies improve, we must adapt and change to meet the more complex needs to guarantee data confidentiality, integrity, and availability.

Summary

In this chapter, we outlined the importance of protecting encryption protocols, processes, and cryptographic techniques. We saw how attacks such as an MiTM attack or a brute-force attack on encrypted data can minimize or negate the effectiveness of these techniques. We discussed Kali Linux, a freely available suite in a hacker's arsenal, which contains hundreds of tools. We then reviewed the dangers of how implementing a weak cipher, such as WEP, can lead to the exposure of data.

We then took a look at some of the attacks against the PKI, which is a framework or infrastructure that is essential for securing data effectively. We saw how various attacks, such as an SSL/TLS strip and DoS attacks, can render the cryptographic processes, elements, and algorithms in PKI useless.

We finished with a discussion on how, over time, there have been advances in computing, with one of these advances being quantum computing. We learned that, because of the power of quantum computing, there is a possibility that our current encryption standards may not be able to withstand an attack. With this concern, we saw how NIST is preparing for this future by selecting post-quantum encryption algorithms that will take us into the next generation of securing data.

Questions

Now it's time to check your knowledge. Select the best response, and then check your answers, which can be found in the *Assessment* section at the end of the book.

1. _____ cache poisoning sends bogus records to a Domain Name System resolver. As a result, when a victim requests an IP address for a website, the server will send the wrong IP address.

    a. ARP

    b. DNS

    c. WEP

    d. MAC

2. _____ spoofing will transmit spoofed ARP messages out on the local area network that falsely reports a malicious actor's MAC as being the victim's address.

    a. ARP

    b. DNS

    c. WEP

    d. MAC

3. WEP is a stream cipher that uses a _____ **initialization vector (IV)** or a 'dummy block' to start the key stream generator.

    a. 24-bytes

    b. 36-bits

    c. 8-bytes

    d. 24-bits

4. _____ was an extension to the Firefox browser that provided an easy way to launch an SSL strip attack.

    a. WEP

    b. Mozilla

    c. Firesheep

    d. Cipher hack

5. A code signing _____ creates a digital signature to validate device drivers, application updates, software, and documents.

   a. certificate

   b. qubit

   c. state machine

   d. wild card

6. In quantum mechanics, the property of _____ is when two particles are interrelated, such that if one changes, the other changes as well, no matter where in the universe the two particles exist.

   a. superposition

   b. entanglement

   c. interference

   d. superstition

7. In quantum mechanics, the property of _____ is the ability to be in multiple states at the same time.

   a. superposition

   b. entanglement

   c. interference

   d. superstition

Further reading

Please refer to the following links for more information:

- To learn more about the vulnerable nature of the 56-bit DES key, visit `https://www.sans.org/reading-room/whitepapers/vpns/day-des-died-722`.

- To view a list of cryptanalysis tools in Kali Linux, go to `https://en.kali.tools/all/?category=crypto`.

- Here is a list of some top password cracking tools in Kali Linux: `https://linuxhint.com/best_kali_linux_password_cracking_tools/`.

- To read more about how a stolen certificate was able to launch a malware attack, visit `https://www.cbronline.com/news/eset-internet-security-firms`.

- Learn more about code signing certificates by going to `https://docs.microsoft.com/en-us/windows-hardware/drivers/install/digital-signatures`.

- To get a better insight into how a code signing certificate works, visit `https://www.venafi.com/education-center/code-signing/what-is-code-signing`.

- To see a list of the top 10 quantum computing companies, visit `https://www.analyticsinsight.net/top-10-quantum-computing-companies-2020/`.

- To read about NIST and the search for post-quantum encryption algorithms, visit `https://www.nist.gov/news-events/news/2019/01/nist-reveals-26-algorithms-advancing-post-quantum-crypto-semifinals`.

Assessments

Chapter 1 – Protecting Data in Motion or at Rest

1. b. 1972
2. a. integrity
3. d. signature
4. d. authentication
5. b. Asymmetric
6. b. Substitution
7. c. transposition

The answer to the secret code in *Figure 1.10*: *Confidentiality is keeping private data private by protecting against unauthorized disclosure*. This may have looked complex, but I substituted Wingdings font for the regular font!

Chapter 2 – The Evolution of Ciphers

1. c. scytale
2. b. substitution
3. a. Vigenère
4. d. 1876
5. a. Enigma
6. d. 01010011
7. a. Lucifer

Chapter 3 – Evaluating Network Attacks

1. d. Passive
2. c. Active
3. a. vector
4. d. appliances
5. c. vulnerability
6. b. vulnerabilities
7. a. Social engineering

Chapter 4 – Introducing Symmetric Encryption

1. d. Feistel
2. a. 1000
3. b. Lucifer
4. c. a single shared key
5. d. shift rows
6. d. Twofish
7. c. padding
8. b. XOR
9. a. CTR
10. d. WPA3

Chapter 5 – Dissecting Asymmetric Encryption

1. b. Diffie-Hellman
2. d. #10
3. c. RSA
4. a. hybrid
5. c. point
6. d. Web of Trust
7. b. HMAC

Chapter 6 – Examining Hash Algorithms

1. b. digest
2. d. HMAC
3. a. big
4. c. deterministic
5. a. Rivest
6. b. Keccak
7. c. CBC-MAC

Chapter 7 – Adhering to Standards

1. b. SHS
2. c. PCI DSS
3. d. HIPAA
4. c. GDPR
5. a. Ransomware
6. b. VoIP
7. a. CALEA

Chapter 8 – Using a Public Key Infrastructure

1. c. keychain
2. a. Kerberos
3. b. Stapling
4. d. CSR
5. a. pinning
6. d. 2048
7. b. X.509
8. c. organization

Chapter 9 – Exploring IPsec and TLS

1. a. PPTP
2. d. SSH
3. b. ESP
4. d. transport
5. c. PFS
6. b. IKE
7. a. handshake
8. c. Record

Chapter 10 – Protecting Cryptographic Techniques

1. b. DNS
2. a. ARP
3. d. 24-bits
4. c. Firesheep
5. a. certificate
6. b. entanglement
7. a. superposition

`Packt.com`

Subscribe to our online digital library for full access to over 7,000 books and videos, as well as industry leading tools to help you plan your personal development and advance your career. For more information, please visit our website.

Why subscribe?

- Spend less time learning and more time coding with practical eBooks and Videos from over 4,000 industry professionals
- Improve your learning with Skill Plans built especially for you
- Get a free eBook or video every month
- Fully searchable for easy access to vital information
- Copy and paste, print, and bookmark content

Did you know that Packt offers eBook versions of every book published, with PDF and ePub files available? You can upgrade to the eBook version at `packt.com` and as a print book customer, you are entitled to a discount on the eBook copy. Get in touch with us at `customercare@packtpub.com` for more details.

At `www.packt.com`, you can also read a collection of free technical articles, sign up for a range of free newsletters, and receive exclusive discounts and offers on Packt books and eBooks.

Other Books You May Enjoy

If you enjoyed this book, you may be interested in these other books by Packt:

CompTIA Security+: SY0-601 Certification Guide – Second Edition

Ian Neil

ISBN: 978-1-80056-424-4

- Get to grips with security fundamentals, from the CIA triad through to IAM
- Explore cloud security and techniques used in penetration testing
- Discover different authentication methods and troubleshoot security issues
- Secure the devices and applications that are used by your company
- Identify and protect against various types of malware and virus
- Protect your environment against social engineering and advanced attacks
- Understand and implement PKI concepts
- Delve into secure application development, deployment, and automation concepts

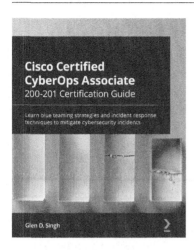

Cisco Certified CyberOps Associate 200-201 Certification Guide

Glen D. Singh

ISBN: 978-1-80056-087-1

- Incorporate security into your architecture to prevent attacks
- Discover how to implement and prepare secure designs
- Identify access control models for digital assets
- Identify point of entry, determine scope, contain threats, and remediate
- Find out how to perform malware analysis and interpretation
- Implement security technologies to detect and analyze threats

Packt is searching for authors like you

If you're interested in becoming an author for Packt, please visit `authors.packtpub.com` and apply today. We have worked with thousands of developers and tech professionals, just like you, to help them share their insight with the global tech community. You can make a general application, apply for a specific hot topic that we are recruiting an author for, or submit your own idea.

Leave a review - let other readers know what you think

Please share your thoughts on this book with others by leaving a review on the site that you bought it from. If you purchased the book from Amazon, please leave us an honest review on this book's Amazon page. This is vital so that other potential readers can see and use your unbiased opinion to make purchasing decisions, we can understand what our customers think about our products, and our authors can see your feedback on the title that they have worked with Packt to create. It will only take a few minutes of your time, but is valuable to other potential customers, our authors, and Packt. Thank you!

Index

S

Made in the USA
Coppell, TX
14 December 2022